More Ways to Use Your Head

PRENTICE-HALL INTERNATIONAL (UK) LIMITED, London
PRENTICE-HALL OF AUSTRALIA PTY. LIMITED, Sydney
PRENTICE-HALL CANADA INC., Toronto
PRENTICE-HALL HISPANOAMERICANA, S.A., Mexico
PRENTICE-HALL OF INDIA PRIVATE LIMITED, New Delhi
PRENTICE-HALL OF JAPAN, INC., Tokyo
PRENTICE-HALL OF SOUTHEAST ASIA PTE. LTD., Singapore
WHITEHALL BOOKS LIMITED, Wellington, New Zealand
EDITORA PRENTICE-HALL DO BRASIL LTDA., Rio de Janeiro

More Ways to Use Your Head

New Methods for Developing
Better Brain Power

STUART LITVAK
A. WAYNE SENZEE

A SPECTRUM BOOK

Prentice-Hall, Inc.,
Englewood Cliffs, New Jersey 07632

Library of Congress Cataloging in Publication Data

Litvak, Stuart.
    More ways to use your head.

    "A Spectrum Book."
    Includes index.
        1. Intellect.   2. Intellect—Problems, exercises,
etc.   3. Self-actualization (Psychology)   4. Self-
actualization (Psychology)—Problems, exercises, etc.
I. Senzee, A. Wayne.   II. Title.
BF431.L532 1985   153   85-3392
ISBN 0-13-601188-8
ISBN 0-13-601170-5 (pbk.)

© 1985 by Prentice-Hall, Inc., Englewood Cliffs, New Jersey 07632

A SPECTRUM BOOK

Printed in the United States of America

10 9 8 7 6 5 4 3 2 1

ISBN 0-13-601188-8

ISBN 0-13-601170-5 {PBK.}

Editorial/production supervision by Marilyn E. Beckford
Cover design by Hal Siegel
Manufacturing buyer: Frank Grieco

This book is available at a special discount when ordered in
bulk quantities. Contact Prentice-Hall, Inc., General
Publishing Division, Special Sales, Englewood Cliffs, N.J. 07632.

Contents

Acknowledgments

The epigram from *Human Options* by Norman Cousins (New York: W. W. Norton & Company, Inc., 1981) is reprinted by permission of the publisher.

The epigraph and the quotation on page 139 from Marcus Aurelius, *Meditations*—trans. Maxwell Staniforth (Penguin Classics, 1964), pp. 46, 115; copyright © Maxwell Staniforth—are reprinted by permission of Penguin Books Ltd.

The quotation on pages 19–20 from Edward deBono, *The Greatest Thinkers* (New York: G. P. Putnam's Sons; London: George Wesdenfeld and Nicolson Limited, 1976), is reprinted by permission.

Scattered quotations from *Reflections*, *Caravan of Dreams*, *The Way of the Sufi*, and *Tales of the Dervishes* by Idries Shah are used by permission of Idries Shah.

The quotation on p. 63 from Jeremy Rifkin with Ted Howard, *Entropy: A New World View*—© 1980 by the Foundation on Economic Trends—is reprinted by permission of Viking Penguin Inc. and Granada Publishing Limited.

The excerpt on page 133 from *Markings* by Dag Hammarskjold, translated by Leif Sjoberg—translation copyright 1964 by Alfred A. Knopf, Inc.—is reprinted by permission of Alfred A. Knopf, Inc.

The human brain is a mirror to infinity. There is no limit to its range, scope, or creative growth. New perspectives lead to new perceptions, just as they clear the way for all sorts of new prospects in human affairs. No one knows what great leaps of achievement may be within the reach of the species once the full potentiality of the mind is developed. As we create an ever-higher sense of our cosmic consciousness, we become aware of our ever-higher possibilities.

Norman Cousins, *Human Options*

Dig within. There lies the well-spring of good: ever dig, and it will ever flow.

Marcus Aurelius, *Meditations*

Introduction

The further we plumb the enfolded mysteries of the brain, the more we realize what a singular and amazing mystery it is. It is unique and enigmatic even in appearance. In its deep, creased mazes run the riddles of the mind itself, and scientists seek the answers to those riddles with perhaps as much high hope as a shaman attempting to trace out a fate with entrails. But to be sure, we cast our lot with the former enterprise, for both human consciousness and destiny are focused in the brain.

Perception, thought, emotion, intuition—these dynamic, daunting, and sometimes awesome experiences are not readily related by the untutored to a three-and-a-half pound, wrinkled, and pickled gray lump of a lab specimen. Like novice caballists, we have just begun to delve into the brain's infinite secrets and fathom its deeper powers. Yet if comedian Woody Allen calls his own witty thinking cap "my second favorite organ," perhaps he is accurately gauging the level of interest many of us have of what goes on inside our own heads.

It is a proposition of this book that it is just this widespread lack of interest in, or unconsciousness of, the brain's incredible capacities for problem solving and self-fulfillment that is, in fact, responsible for our species' collectively behaving like a high-IQ amnesiac, destructively reacting against his environment, his fellow man, and himself. At least fifty local wars now in progress around the globe, nuclear bombs pointed everywhere on earth, mass starvation and disease, plant and animal decimation, degradation of the environment, air and water pollution . . . the "rap sheet" is long. And, more alarming, these unhappy conditions seem to be taken as almost inevitable by large numbers of us.

Paradoxically, we tend to be unduly enthralled with ersatz versions of brain power, memory feats, calculating abilities, boggling psychic phenomena, and such. Today's biggest preoccupation is, of course, the computer. While the systems comparison between the human brain and artificial intelligence (AI) is useful and frequently stressed, let us here underscore their rather stupendous differences.

A human brain contains between 10 billion and 100 billion neurons, or nerve cells. The neuron, like the components of a computer, functions by way of (bio-) electrical impulses. According to William Shoemaker of the Salk Institute in La Jolla, California, the average neuron "is as complex as an entire small computer." Which makes the entire human brain, with 10 to 100 billion computers, an ultracomputer to truly boggle the mind. In contrast to modern AI, which historically dates back but fifty years or so, the human organ of intelligence can be traced back at least 250 million years to its rudimentary origin in primitive organisms. So with eons of accumulated knowledge and survival wisdom stored in its some 4.3 billion brains or supercomputers, why are so many people behaving like a starving, disconsolate man who does not realize that the becoming hat sitting so heavily upon his head contains such an unimaginably rich horn of plenty? The answer is quite plain: We don't know how to use all our brain power. And many of us who actually get around to pondering it think that the horn of plenty is but a fistful of nuts and raisins.

Thus such pastimes as doing crossword puzzles, solving math problems, playing "logic games," wiseacreing and practicing one-upsmanship are usually considered vigorous exercising of intelligence. But would anyone consider the ability to do cartwheels necessary for escaping from a prison? Well . . . perhaps these pastimes are valuable as distractions . . . the fact is that these kinds of diversions only strengthen areas of the brain *already* established, i.e., the more or less active 20 percent. In terms of potential neural development, however, the brain may barely be in embryo. Consider: roughly just 5 percent of the average brain's neurons are functionally active in cognitive/emotive processes. Furthermore, most of these fledgling cells have only a few hundred circuit connections to neighboring cells, while a paltry minority have developed upwards into the thousands, as much as twenty thousand. Conclusion: Mentally, most of us are malnourished, settling for a peanut (a happy idea) once in a while, though each of us could be developing a chock-full larder. Far-fetched as it may seem, this metaphor could be literally true for the world's 4.3 billion dormant superbrains, for the possibilities of the brain's development and evolution are endless.

More Ways to Use Your Head has the same premise as its predecessor, *Use Your Head:* Any functioning person can tap at least 80 percent more of his or her brain power and creativity than he or she ordinarily keeps tucked away under his or her cranial cap. Unlike other self-help manuals, however, this book avoids the facile assumptions of most how-to-do-it advice, where the process of preparation and orientation is either minimized or ignored altogether. To break into a larder or out of a prison requires first a general knowledge (overview) of the situation and one's present capacities to optimize every advantage at one's disposal. Following a set of instructions, viewing pictures and exercising may be aids at certain points, but they may actually be detrimental if relied upon at the wrong times. Have you ever heard of anyone becoming a black-belt karatist by studying a handbook?

Exploiting unused areas of your brain requires both a different perspective and a different approach. We begin by having new experiences, starting with the new information that this book contains. We learn what sorts of things *block* perception and experience and how to recognize them. Challenging narrow attitudes, mental sets, automatic assumptions, beliefs, values, even pet interests and theories can be worthwhile. *What* you think and *how* you go about thinking it are really quite intriguing dynamics. And beyond all this are yet more vital mental faculties, which seem to have little connection to everyday concerns—wisdom, intuition, "the language of the heart"—but which can indeed expand and deepen your mind.

Naturally, just reading this book will not make you a superthinker. You will have to act, in a balanced way, on the information given day by day. Do your best to apply the principles described in the following pages in a reasonably consistent way without setting up an arbitrary timetable or being too hard on yourself. Relaxation is the first basic. You can then begin to make the best use of the new experiences and ideas that will help you in provoking your brain along unfamiliar and presently untrodden pathways.

Happy pathfinding!

Chapter One

The Incomplete Brain

It is a common misperception that substantial damage to the brain inevitably results in blithering idiocy. However, abundant research shows the contrary. It also helps us to understand how the whole, unimpaired brain works. Remarkably, in numerous cases many kinds of diseases and injuries do not debilitate the victim to a marked degree.

A variety of medical findings and brain surgery with monkeys and humans validate the old saw that "it's not how much you've got upstairs but how you use it." How about half a brain? People who have had half their brain surgically removed (*hemispherectomy*) because of spreading cancer or tumors are able to carry on fulfilling lives, as before the removal, with but minor deficiency. When the right hemisphere is removed, "left-brain" persons can still use language efficiently, converse, read, and write as well as do basic arithmetic in their heads. Most tasks requiring orderly, sequential thought are performed relatively well. Interestingly, when these individuals do talk, their expression and intonation tend to be rather flat and inflectionless, more "robotlike" than before.

A bigger surprise is that the right-side hemispherectomy can be performed on some people without their noticing any later effects at all! Patients often insist that absolutely everything is the same. But follow-up studies reveal that these left-brainers have lost some touch of personality, intuition, imagination, and insight and have residual trouble with spatial tasks. The denial of these measurable shortfalls may be the left hemisphere's overcompensation for the loss of its "other half" or some innate egoism in its own cognitive nature. Perhaps both.

After left-hemispherectomy the right-brain patient has marginal difficulties with verbal and numerical activities although usually not enough to prevent him from functioning adequately day by day. In all other respects—social interactions, recreation, art and music appreciation, spatial tasks, and so on—he or she gets on quite well. There is no excessive "spacing out," no quirks of personality, providing the person is treated normally.

The plain and important conclusion of split-brain studies is that our organ of intelligence is a versatile, flexible, and self-regenerative entity indeed. The two sides of the brain overlap considerably in function and can compensate for each other to maintain at least social standards for "normalcy." Writing in *New Scientist* magazine, Stan Gooch, who has worked with outstanding split-brain people in England and South Africa, concludes that "each side" tends to specialize in certain functions but doesn't lose the ability to take over all if the need arises."[1] A widely accepted hypothesis for this phenomenon is that nature has wisely provided us with a "spare" brain. So not only is half a brain better than none, it looks as if it is almost as good as a whole one.

What about no brain at all? If by *brain* we mean the cerebral cortex, that handful of furrowed gray tissue that fills most of our cranium and is considered by most experts to be the cradle of all higher thought processes, then we can even be practically brainless and still be smart. For on record are hydrocephalus victims with no cortex detected on their brain scans who scored 120 and above on IQ tests and others who are A and B students in school. Neurologist John Lorber of Sheffield University, who has studied these cases, believes that the cortex may be over-rated in brain functioning, and that conceivably the "deeper, more primitive brain structures hold more sway over intelligence."[2] Another possibility is that around 5 percent of the cortex of the hydrocephalics studied was in fact intact. Which would partly contradict Lorber.

The meaning of these findings is beginning to unfold, as if out of the fissured depths of the brain itself. Still, questions may be popping out of the crevices of your own gray matter. What is all of that extra brain really for then? To keep us from looking pin-headed? To cushion whatever it is that does the hard thinking? These are not facetious queries. To get possible answers, though, let us retrace our steps back to the concept of "normal," not in brain size or structure but in how the brain is used by masses of people.

Speaking in percentages, one authority, Dr. Win Wenger, estimates that we use less than 1 percent of our brain capacity.[3] From that we easily deduce that if we were to lose 95 percent of our cerebral cortex (as in hydrocephalus), we quite possibly would lose no brain power at all. Indeed, if such an occurrence forced us to make more use of what gray matter was left, we might end up more intelligent than before, consonant or not with our IQ score—thus hydrocephalics who score 120+. How in headbone could one make do with 5 percent or less of his or her potential smart? The answer is as discernible as water on the brain: because the "normal" requirements of everyday life for "normal" people make little or no demand upon the remaining 95 percent or more of their gray matter languishing in dormancy. The majority of us lead a largely unvaried, routinized life. The generally few changes we are obliged to make in our agendas simply do not break enough new mental ground to change the percentages or increase our overall intelligence.

Because our daily routine involves a dozen or so different activities we are apt to think that our brain is being fully exercised, especially when we experience stress. But stress is not mere fatigue, and the exhaustion we feel at the end of a busy day could be caused by repetitious overload of small areas of the brain rather than by overwork of the whole organ. Many routines do not seem especially strenuous, but they can take a heavy toll over extended periods, resulting in the familiar "burn-out" syndrome caused by continual tension and boredom. As numerous stress experts are wont to point out, very often the most stressful activities are those that are repetitive (we might add *unconscious*) and not excluding some we consider diversional.

The "normal" requirements of everyday life for most people are actually quite minimal, even if they are time and energy consuming.

Let us play the part of a private eye and "tail" a randomly picked American worker for fourteen hours; for a touch more personal, call him or her Sal: (Sounds a lot like . . ."):

- 6:30 A.M.: Out of bed, toilet, shower, clothes on, breakfast, read the newspaper or watch TV news, off to work.

- 8:00 A.M. to 4:30 P.M.: One more of about 250 relatively homogeneous workdays of the year. Half hour off for lunch, same time. Quitting time, drive back home.

- 5:00 P.M.: Back home. Drop on sofa, fall asleep (the reason Sal didn't stop off for a couple beers or some shopping on the way home).

- 6:15 P.M.: Wake up . . . Rats, news on TV half over . . . Too late, too tired to fix dinner—sandwich again or eat out? . . . This single life not what it's cracked up to be . . . Should I get a cat or a dog?

- 7:00 P.M. to 10:30 P.M.: TV watching and telephone chat. Get ready for bed—oh-oh, out of bread and coffee for morning. Dash to convenience mart. Finally to bed.

We admit that this is a pretty skeletal sketch, not identical for all people. Details aside, however, do you see much of your own lifestyle in Sal's habit-laden activities? Of course there are some peripheral variations in Sal's routine, but most of them are themselves too habitual and minor to alter the regular grind: Friday or Saturday he or she may frequent a bar or nightclub or go to a movie. Perhaps love-making at expected intervals. Saturday or Sunday is usually errand day for Sal (housekeeping, yardwork, laundry, shopping, car maintenance). Socializing and recreation usually slotted on the clock and calendar: tennis, jogging, golf (maybe miniature), concert, club meeting. For marrieds the domestic schedule is tighter than for dependent-less singles, who commonly spend their extra time contacting the opposite sex—bar hopping, dating. Possibly there is church on Sunday morning.

Reviewing such an agenda and putting it in the context of a lifetime, we have little room to doubt that the role of Sal could be stood in by a wonderfully well programmed robot. "But," you may object, "what about the personality, the feeling, the thinking that accompany these routines?" Actually, those are less complex and more automated than you might have been previously led to believe. If you are employed as a clerk, office manager, bureaucrat, or factory worker, for instance, most of what you do involves virtually the same basic stimuli and required responses day after day. Personality and feeling probably spend most of the time in the washroom or express themselves during coffee breaks. How much thinking is ipso facto there if original thoughts or actions are discouraged by your superiors because they might slow—at least temporarily—work output? Real thinking is a rare bird, called on only in alien or emergency situations. Most jobs are laid out for speed and the largest possible production quota, elimination of unfamiliar factors being a top priority in the interest of smooth execution—that is to say, "efficiency." Novel ideas and the spontaneous kind of personality that usually produces them are avoided, sometimes reprimanded. So far you may be having trouble swallowing the idea that large chunks of your life could be handled by a robot. Others, perhaps, but not "spontaneous me." Nonetheless, artificial-intelligence (AI) experts have designed computer programs that can even copy human pastimes considered by all of us to be extemporaneous and not at all machinelike. The silicon cyberneticians have discovered that behavior in our diversional settings is just as prescribed and predictable as our workaday mode. Sports, for example, are highly ritualistic; one contest is a generic variation on the model or ideal face-off, perfection measured in terms of promotion and gate receipts.

The unvarnished truth is that masses of people are unconsciously stuck in the niches of routine as so many polyps in a coral reef. AI analysts have confirmed with their techniques that human behavior in most situations can be prognosticated, laden as they are with key stimuli and standard responses. In AI argot, *script/frame/slot* analysis defines the setting (objects, people) of a generic-type activity and the prototypical conduct that inevitably takes place within it. A *frame* is a cognitive schematic of all (or certain) features of the situation, while the *script* alludes to the repertoire of expected behaviors to which the participants are limited by the framework. A *slot* is a specific subfeature of the frame elements.

A script/frame scenario is set up by *expectation*, based on past experience within the generic situation. Take the example of dining out: We enter a restaurant unknown to use, but expect and usually find tables, menus, waiters, and so on. We are sure that a certain *sequence of events* will take place: We will be seated (perhaps by a hostess) at a vacant, cleared table; a waitress will greet us with the menus and water; she will disappear while we decide upon our meal, and so it will go until we ultimately pay our check to the cashier and exit. This would be the average café version. But whether it is dinner at Sardi's or lunch at McDonald's, each class of eatery has a generic script/frame. And all this time we thought *generic* meant only a certain nondescript aisle in the supermarket stocked with black-and-white-labeled items. In the script/frame of the supermarket itself that aisle would be only a subfeature, and grabbing an item or two in an inconspicuous manner would constitute filling in a subfeature *slot* of your greater grocery shopping. There is a script/frame for every public outing you can think of, and—who knows?—perhaps our private lives include more role playing than we think.

What does all of this presage for our social and cerebral future? Computer-operated robots are now available that can efficiently perform as butlers and maids, run offices and factories, edit your writing while you are at it (word processors), stand in at certain levels for teachers and counselors . . . their accomplishments go on and on. In a *Scientific American* anthology called *The Mechanization of Work*, articles on the mechanizing of agriculture, mining, commerce (finance, distribution, and transport), office procedure, manufacturing, and design engineering make clear that artificial intelligence is rendering laboring man and woman obsolete.[4] By calling up only 5 to 20 percent of his or her brain power, can thinking man or woman be far behind?

Actually, the *potential* of the human brain is light-years beyond what the most sophisticated computer can mimic. When compared with the brain's vast neural network, as blown up by microphotography, computer circuitry waxes less awesome and somewhat more Tinker Toy–like. The brain has anywhere from 10 billion to 100 billion neurons, and the number of inter-connections between all these brain cells calculates to some-where around 10,000,000,000 (taken as the average brain) followed by 800 more naughts. In comparison, the estimated number of atoms in the known universe is a mere 10 followed by 100 naughts. It is no cloud-floating platitude that the brain, measured by the scale of its basic unit, is a universe unto itself of practically incomprehensible magnitude.

Bioelectrically the brain functions by way of neurotrans-mitters and scores of other chemicals. Dr. David Samuels of the Weizmann Institute in New York estimates that there are between 10,000 and 1,000,000 different chemical reactions occurring in the brain virtually every minute.[5] This really awesome sphere of apparently infinite potential has prompted one brain researcher, Michael Phelps of UCLA, to dub it "an ungodly complex system."[6] But better, perhaps, to think of its immensely wasted powers as ungodly.

Translating all this cerebral potential into personal devel-opment and completion begins with the question: What are we actually capable of? Or what is entailed when we excel the norm? To begin with, we are far less *creative* in every facet of everyday life than we could be if we were to develop our brain/minds beyond their present limits. A widespread fallacy about creativity is that it is an inborn gift rather than a capacity that can be cultivated. Another one is that it is aligned with spe-cialization of some sort—artistic creativity, inventive creativity, social creativity—and is not generally looked on as a total way of life. *Productivity* is the magic word in our object-oriented, consumer society. Creativity is not limited simply by what we can see, touch, hear, or smell (tangibles) but can include intangibles as well: love, unselfish ideas, ideals, feelings, and genuine spiritual inclinations. You can be more creative in anything, from redecorating the interior of your home to reacting more constructively to certain of your spouse's shortcomings to practicing making more balanced evaluations of your life overall and adjusting toward improvement accordingly.

Closely related to the ability to live creatively is the knack for *lateral thinking*, a descriptive coined by Dr. Edward deBono to depict a mode of thinking qualitively different from the option-minimizing form of traditional linear cogitation based on "logic" (which is illogical in much day-to-day application). Lateral thinking, which often seems illogical on cursory consideration, is, on the contrary, a tremendously potent problem-solving method when used efficiently. It is more concerned with the generation of new ideas than with the refinement of old ones, with possibilities rather than certainties. Lateral thinking does not replace logic in its necessary functions but instead complements it as an exploratory skill. The useful beauty of lateral thinking is that any coherent person can learn how to do it. High IQ and higher education are not essential. Exposure to the numerous techniques devised by deBono helps to stimulate this latent facility so that it can be operative on demand where logic-based thinking is inadequate.

Intuition is another dormant faculty in most people. Broadly defined, it refers to all of our thinking processes not accessible to verbal analysis. Intuition is the spontaneous feeling of truth, without conscious inference. Although it is often and erroneously equated by common belief with the flights and fantasies of imagination, it is actually grounded in objective experience. "Vibes," "gut feelings," and "hunches" are false or true depending on their ultimate verification. Recent studies reveal that many successful business people rely heavily upon intuition, frequently making correct decisions in defiance of logic or "fact." Other studies of renowned artists, thinkers, and inventors show that most of their finest accomplishments (if not all of them) are the progeny of interplay between intuition and imagination. Like general creativity and lateral thinking, intuition can be provoked into arousal in all of us, beyond its occasional stirrings. Furthermore, it can be developed to produce "genius" in individuals thought to be of mediocre, or even inferior, intelligence. *Awakening Intuition* by Frances E. Vaughn is an excellent source of information on the subject. As Vaughn points out, "Awakening intuition is really about learning to trust yourself."[7] And the late eclectical genius R. Buckminster Fuller saw intuition as that process in the mind that can seek and find out what is "unknown and unexpectedly existent," that is, "generalized principles" of the cosmos that go unwatched for and unperceived by surface consciousness.

Which brings us to another largely atrophied process in humans: *perception.* Conditioning and too rigid pattern thinking cause overfiltering of environmental information, a process that does not fit the brain's deeply embedded patterns. That is especially true of visual screening but also involves the reinforcing complex of the other senses: touch, smell, hearing, and taste. The "sixth sense," and perhaps other elusive psychic dynamics, may play important roles as well. John Berger notes in his book *Ways of Seeing,* "In the Middle Ages when men believed in the physical existence of Hell the sight of fire must have meant something different from what it means today."[8] Culture is the first-order perception maker and, as such, has been extensively probed by such thinkers as Edward T. Hall (*Beyond Culture, The Hidden Dimension, The Silent Language*) and Weston La Barre (*The Human Animal*).[9] The way we have been trained to see and sense the world around us colors our perceptions through cerebral shifts still not fully understood. Consider: A study was conducted in which slides were shown to viewers to evaluate how reliable "eye-witness" court testimony is. One slide was of a black man with empty hands conversing with a white man who was holding a razor. A majority of the white viewers later recalled the black man as holding the razor. There are other cases of entire groups of people not seeing something that is materially present and vice versa, owing to their belief system. (See chapter 4, "Blindside.") By gaining insight into our conditioning, thought patterns, assumptions,

13

and hidden biases we can steadily enlarge our scope of perception.

For creativity to be tapped in toti, the foregoing aptitudes must be cultivated to the maximum, in a balanced and essentially conscious manner. Once propagated, however, they become "second nature," or, perhaps more accurately, "first nature." Certain individuals have contacted, in a more or less erratic fashion, their deeper resources of lateral thinking, perception, and intuition and are therefore a few lengths out in front of those who have not, which is most of us. Research from a school of psychology called humanistic/transpersonal indicates that fewer than 1 percent of the total population, in their inner selves, have matured into the most fulfilling degree of adulthood. These fortunate individuals were referred to as "self-actualizers" by the late psychologist Abraham Maslow, who studied them throughout his long and productive career.

Such popular books as Gail Sheehy's *Passages: Predictable Crises of Adult Life*[10] are apt to give us the impression that the only stages in life are childhood, adolescence, young adulthood, midlife, and decline into old age. It is true that this agenda holds for most people, but what are the developmental rungs to self-actualization for those who do attain it? Maslow identified our prerequisites: physiological needs, safety, love or belongingness, and self-esteem. Self-actualization is achieved after realization of these. At the lowest level, the individual satisfies the basic drives and needs, such as food, shelter, and sex. Then he or she pursues and secures the safety of group cohesion: family, friends, community. When security is ensured, the individual expends his or her energy in obtaining self-esteem by way of other-consensus of his or her personal worth. But after that is established, the person still feels incompletion at the center of his or her Self and often attempts to fill the void simply by gaining yet more community esteem and self-esteem.

The self-actualized person, according to Maslow, has passed beyond the need for confirmation from society. He or she has made contact with something deeper, more vital within himself or herself, which nourishes and energizes, even in the face of hostility or indifference from others. This 1 percent of humanity is looked upon as qualitively different from the remaining 99 percent and is usually not well understood as such. Nevertheless, self-actualizers are commonly celebrated and idolized, if only after their death. As examples Maslow cites Schweitzer, Einstein, Lincoln, Eleanor Roosevelt, Martin Buber, Longfellow, Goethe, Emerson, and Benjamin Franklin, among others. The common denominator of all these personages is the absence of neurosis or any kind of mental illness and the manifestation of maturity, responsibility, objectivity, unselfishness, superior perception, conscience, good judgment, decisiveness, knowledgeability, broad interests, humility, self-understanding, dedication, discipline, and of course creativity. Peripheral qualities of flexibility, spontaneity, openness, courage, and willingness to risk mistakes and to listen are also readily displayed by this minority.

Admirable and healthy as all of the above qualities are, they are yet but nurtured by-products of certain intense inner states characterized by a sense of awe, rapture, ecstasy, bliss, and intense happiness. At the time of these experiences, perhaps lasting but a few moments, the self-actualizer feels "at his or her best," the total feeling being unforgettable. While these "peak experiences" are not exclusive to this group, self-actualizers have more than the average share of them. Their "oceanic" sensations are frequently described as mystical, though they seem to occur no more often in nominally religious people than in others.

Preceding Maslow by over half a century was the brilliant research of Richard Maurice Bucke, M.D. Subtitled *A Classic Investigation of the Development of Man's Relation to the Infinite, Cosmic Consciousness*[11] was the outgrowth of Bucke's own stunning "peak experience" at the age of thirty-five. Bucke spent the remainder of his life conducting in-depth analyses of remarkable individuals, past and present. Years later Maslow did the same thing. Coincidentally (since Maslow was initially unaware of Bucke's work), some of the same people Maslow studied had been investigated earlier by Bucke. They included, for example, the poets Whitman and Emerson. Bucke believed, however, that total self-potential could be realized *before* age sixty, a possibility that Maslow seems not to have considered. Bucke profiled such figures as Buddha, Jesus, Paul, Plotinus, Mohammed, Dante, John Yepes (St. John of the Cross), Francis Bacon, William Blake, Moses, Lao-Tze, Socrates, Roger Bacon, and Rama Krishna Paramahansa.

Whereas Maslow's interest in self-actualized individuals did not go beyond psychology proper, Bucke's inquiry was within the framework of conscious—that is, self-directed—evolution. His criteria of attainment to the state of cosmic consciousness included moral elevation; intellectual illumination; sense of immortality; loss of the fear of death; loss of the sense of sin; sudden, instant awakening; charisma; and the acquisition of a "cosmic sense." Bucke did not see these states as bestowing omniscience or infallability on the person experiencing them but rather as the dynamic hallmarks of his having "reached a higher mental level." Such people, he maintained, live life to a degree of fullness unknown by ordinary humanity and extract its meaning and interests from "totally different points of view." Therefore, they are at least one developmental progression above humans en masse, both morally and mentally.

On closer consideration we are tempted to interpret Bucke's categories of mental advancement as indicative of something beyond even self-actualization. We might call it *self-transcendence*. In a recent book, *Eye To Eye*,[12] Ken Wilber identifies self-transcendence as the highest plane of spirituality accessible to living persons. In religious parlance, this "ultimate state of consciousness" is equivalent to the Kingdom of God, Brahman, Buddha-Nature, and Absolute.

Mystical states, in common assumption, are associated with irrationality, but this notion is, in reality, the polar opposite of the truth. For the authentic mystical or visionary experience instills objectivity in the mind, in contrast to the bogus experience, which increases emotionality and subjectivity. In his definitive work, *The Varieties of Religious Experience*, William James dispels the popular idea of transcendental states as pathological. Upon review of the descriptive accounts of mystical experiences of numerous remarkable men, James concludes that such experiences may "be after all the truest of insights into the meaning of this life."[13]

In his investigation of mystics and mystical systems, James treats what may be the most influential current among the various traditions, Sufism. He rightly states: "We Christians know little of Sufism, for its secrets are disclosed only to those initiated." As secretive and exclusive as that may sound, authentic Sufism operates through an exceptionally open format in non-oppressive societies, its only requirement for study being that of capacity. In *The Sufis*,[14] Idries Shah takes us beyond the Maslovian model into realms of consciousness and achievement undreampt of by even the most optimistic of us. Shah describes, in an annotation called "Seven Men," seven states of higher human development, of which the first reflects the vast majority of humanity. His descriptions of stages two and three may possibly parallel Maslow's self-actualization states, although the subsequent levels are unknown to almost all of us. The fully realized attributes of these stages include real mental integration, extradimensional experience, completion, objective understanding, and love on a sublime plane.

Many people find it hard for their logical selves to accept that there are ranges of human experience and development far beyond the norm around them. Yet genuine logic and skepticism do not deny assertions out of hand, especially those supported by documented studies such as the foregoing. All of the achiever profiles listed can be checked and verified, biographies, autobiographies, hagiographies, and "confessions" consulted. Doing so will in all probability convince skeptics that the "norm" is only a statistical average, actually depicting a "subnormality" in terms of total cerebral potential.

Arguing that genius is inherited, that accomplishment is the product of random fortuities in the brain and the environment, does not square with the evidence as it has been researched. The purpose of this book is to provide practical information and suggestions in a nonformulistic framework, after first furthering the reader's general awareness of the conditions, opportunities, and problems involved in exploiting one's cerebral capacity. The initial objective is to realistically grasp one's true possibilities, minimizing the elements that prevent the perception of those possibilities.

We strongly advise you to follow up on the information in the following pages by consulting as many as possible of the source books cited. Absorption of the material will thereby be more efficient and perhaps more rapid. Preparation is paramountly important, prerequisite to applying the various concepts and principles to your everyday behavior and experience.

Notes

1. Stan Gooch, *New Scientist*, cited in *Omni*, September 1981, p. 45.
2. John Lorber, *World Medicine*, cited in *Omni*, June 1981, p. 53.
3. Win Wenger, *How to Increase Your Intelligence* (New York: Bobbs-Merrill, 1975), p. 36.
4. Scientific American Reader, ed., *The Mechanization of Work* (San Francisco: W. H. Freeman, 1982).
5. David Samuels, cited in Tony Buzan, *Use Both Sides of Your Brain* (New York: E. P. Dutton & Co., 1976), p. 17.
6. Phelps, Michael, "The Mysteries of the Brain, *Newsweek*, Feb. 7, 1983, p. 41.
7. Francis E. Vaughn, *Awakening Intuition* (Garden City, N.Y.: Anchor/Doubleday, 1979), p. v.
8. John Berger, *Ways of Seeing* (New York: Penguin Books, 1972), p. 8.
9. Edward T. Hall, *Beyond Culture* (Garden City, N.Y.: Anchor/Doubleday, 1976); *The Hidden Dimension* (Garden City, N.Y.: Anchor/Doubleday, 1969); *The Silent Language*, (Garden City, N.Y.: Doubleday, 1959); Weston La Barre, *The Human Animal* (Chicago: University of Chicago Press, 1911).
10. Gail Sheehy, *Passages: Predictable Crises of Adult Life* (New York: Bantam, 1977).
11. Richard Maurice Bucke, *Cosmic Consciousness* (New York: E. P. Dutton & Co., 1901).
12. Ken Wilber, *Eye To Eye* (Garden City, N.Y.: Anchor/Doubleday, 1983).
13. William James, *The Varieties of Religious Experience* (New York: New American Library, 1958), p. 323.
14. Idries Shah, *The Sufis* (Garden City, N.Y.: Anchor/Doubleday, 1964).

Chapter Two

Cognitive Traps

Little Sal was a chronic questioner who regularly exasperated adults with his numerous and observant queries. He was a nemesis of the final answer.

One day at school, while the teacher was giving Sal's class a geography lesson with the world globe, all of the pupils crowded around.

"What would happen if somebody fell off the world?" a six-year-old girl wanted to know.

"That can't happen, Brenda," answered the teacher. "Gravity holds us down."

Just then a small spider scuttled out from under the base of the globe and disappeared down the edge of the desk.

"Can people crawl out of the bottom of it when they get scared," asked Sal, "like bugs?"

Psychologist and inventor Edward deBono has done a great deal of thinking about thinking. In his underrated book, *The Greatest Thinkers*, he writes:

Most thinkers never define their universe but take it for granted that their thinking lies in the general universe of "man" or

We all use logic to some degree, in better or worse forms. The general problem with this thinking tool, however, is that we often use it on tasks for which it is inadequate—the "nailing jelly to a tree" fallacy. Less ludicrously, the misapplication is more akin to trying to drive a ten-penny nail into concrete or mistaking glue for varnish. Most of us know what the results will be in both cases. Yet the average person has no inkling of the heavy blemishes misplaced logic leaves on his or her mind. Intellectuals are not exceptionally wise to cognitive pitfalls and frequently fall into them, even in their specialties.

An example of a thinker mistaking part for whole was the Greek geometrist Euclid. He reasoned that the entire universe was one of intersecting lines on a flat, two-dimensional surface and that his geometry was applicable everywhere. These assumptions are contained in his first axioms (premises). His logical reasoning was impeccable, and thus many thinkers after him accepted his system as valid for the total universe. But as later discovery proved, it became invalid when applied to the surface of spheres and in three dimensions. His "truths" turned out untrue inversely to the fact of the earth's curvature.

We consciously or unconsciously (usually the latter) begin with certain assumptions (*axioms* in formal logic) and build upon these additional assumptions (*postulates* and *corollaries*). The positing of the original assumption or axiom is known as first stage thinking. Further deductions and development of the system is known as second stage thinking—no major feat. For two thousand years after Euclid plane geometry was a mental trench out of which metaphysicians, theologians, cosmologists, and almost everybody else could not see. For all practical and nonpractical purposes, everyone was flat minded.

Comprehending the error of taking a lesser world to be an absolute or general universe opens up a new perspective on our own mental horizons. Just as later geometries took in the realities of the third (depth) and fourth (time) dimensions of this world, so our minds should strive for larger truths and not mistake any level of understanding for the final one. Too much of the time we think and act like everyday Euclideans, schooled as we are in limited ideas and boxed-in logic. It's like thinking that our solar system is the whole cosmos without realizing that there are billions of other planetary systems in our Milky Way galaxy alone, not to mention those in other galaxies, of which there are millions.

We should never underestimate the chances for error in attempting to extrapolate a facet (a "fact") of reality into a greater truth, particularly when our reasoning is not based on verifiable experience. It was this kind of untried yet instituted "truth" that prevented pre-Galilean astronomers and theological cosmologists from imagining that the earth might not be the center of the universe or even of the solar system. If it hadn't been for men such as Magellan and Columbus who dared to test these fixed mental models and beliefs in the actual world, humans might have shrunk from all inner and outer horizons and retreated into their psychic caves.

In spite of the relativistic limits of our knowledge and experience, it is common practice for the majority of us to stake our beliefs and affairs, and thus our world view, in a personally specialized universe, forgetting that there are bigger—and perhaps better—worlds outside. Consciously or unconsciously (usually the latter), we begin with certain assumptions and base our actions on them. If our first assumptions and actions are grounded in experiential knowledge, then their effects will be auspicious in proportion to their validity—if not . . . well, look at so many of the events that make up the daily news. Better yet, review one of your own memorable faux pas in this light. We are so used to taking notice of the mistakes of others that we seldom stop to consider similar cases of our own. The common denominator is usually the tendency to "mistake part for whole," to perceive things in too piecemeal a fashion.

CRIME STOP

Persuaded to attend a community "Conference On Crime," Sal heard all manner of harangues from far left and right field and everything in between on "how to stem the rising tide of crime" in the city. Toward the end of the evening Sal's unbroken silence was taken note of and input was requested of him, nay demanded. Reluctantly, he stood up, then riveted the audience's attention by barking out, "Rehabilitation and Re-Education! . . . . no mollycoddling offenders! . . . full victim compensation! . . . no nonsense expedition of justice! . . . more involvement on the personal level! . . ."

"Come now," someone interrupted, "all of those solutions have already been proposed tonight—can't you add any new ideas?"

"Allow me to finish," continued Sal. "Are these 'solutions' *really* solutions? The only new idea I can add is that they are not. These are, in fact, but assumed remedies for the syndrome of a social ill which is much larger than the single symptom we call 'crime'. Therefore, the working 'solution' to crime, I believe is not to seek solutions to the crime symptom but to recognize the greater syndrome and its origins rooted in the human mind."

Since we have brushed the subject of crime, let us take it as an example of a major social ill that is exacerbated by our hardheaded misuse of logic. A child with a pair of scissors may go to work on the curtains when he runs out of construction paper, even if he has been told what the scissors are *not* for. Adults do no end of damage with their mental (and physical) tools, repeating their mistakes time and again.

Responding in interviews to the information that increasing the punishment for inmate misbehavior correlated to an overall increase in antisocial acts and violence, prison guards concluded, after many discussions and meetings, that the answer to the problem was "to punish the increased violence." Now that is sticking to your guns so tightly that it indicates you could have glued them to your hands. Yet crime continues on the upswing after centuries of the punishment method. You might need to examine our first stage thinking here and ask *how* intensifying punishment increases antisocial responses not only inside prison but outside it. That, in turn, could provoke us into wondering what elements in the society are contributing to the high recidivism rate (repeat offenses and reincarceration) of hardened convicts as well as what the particular motivations of the "one-timers" are. Such queries have in fact been made periodically, but nearly all of them have fallen short of comprehensive answers. Is it possible that the carrots currently being offered in the form of inmate rehabilitation are being accepted mainly as bribery in the face of the stick's brittle ineffectiveness?

To better understand crime, criminologists (and all of us) will have to emerge from their specialized universe and question their assumptions about the causes and management of crime. Behavioral principles in broader contexts may have to be studied in depth by the specialists. For instance, if you aren't aware, B. F. Skinner, in using punishment with rats in the 1950s, found that once a habit or pattern was established, punishment was relatively unsuccessful in extinguishing that behavior. It might temporarily stop it, but the old behavior pattern would eventually return.

Skinner's studies and many of those of his successors have revealed more than just the effects of punishment. In order for the rats to learn the original habits (e.g., pressing levers in order to obtain food), they had to be extensively deprived in the first place—they had to be hungry. Extrapolating back to human crime, a constructive question (instead of simply asking how we should punish criminals) would be how criminals are prompted to begin their illegal acts in the first place. What might they be deprived of and why? This query opens up a whole new social universe for our examination: What elements in the very fundament of our society are fostering crime? Why do some communities such as those of the modernized Scandinavians and the primitive aborigines have low crime rates? Societies are composed of individuals, and what characteristics in those individuals are responsible for the kinds of social structuring that provide the breeding ground for crime? The point is, again, that until we look at our fondest assumptions we will not make much progress in solving the problems that are being caused or aggravated by them.

Helping to keep us pinned down to our premises and special universes are what are known as concept fixations. Dr. deBono is one of a number of thinkers who have emphasized how "words and names" inhibit human perception. He maintains that overreliance on classification systems results in conceptual immobility and entrapment. Emergencies and unexpected situations have a way of forcing us out of these word-ordered straitjackets. DeBono recounts an illustrative tale of a bomber pilot who encountered problems with his controls during the flight home. A thorough check by the crew led to the discovery that the hydraulic system was leaking. Fluid to refill the system could not be found. At last a crew member did what came naturally, but instead of doing it in his pants he did it into the hydraulic system. Of course, humans have their own hydraulic systems, but as deBono notes, they are categorically unthought of as such by the average person in usual circumstances.

Think of the numerous kinds of social and personal difficulties that could be discharged out of our ailing systems by similar exercising of *lateral thinking*. (deBono's term). How about the congested approaches to the traffic problem in our large cities? The *idée fixe* solution is to build more expressways. However, the accelerating expense of construction, head-on disruption of personal lives, uprooting of families, destruction of many attractive residences and successful businesses, and pollution make this "solution" far from ideal. But the *concept* is freeways, and more freeways yet. Alternatives are not generated because the *focus* on freeways is too strong. Letting go of this fixation might allow us to catch hold of other possibilities, which singularly or collectively could lead to a more humanistic and satisfactory solution to the snarling problem. Interestingly, many of the answers arise from individuals themselves. No governmental agency can as yet force you to take up walking, bicycling, motor cycling, or bus riding. Car pooling has demonstrated modest success. And since traffic is most congested during rush hours, (about 8 A.M. and 5 P.M.), another conceivable adjustment is to get employers to stagger work schedules when and where feasible. A little lateral thinking can go a long way.

The application of lateral thinking to improve the conditions in our most private lives is so laden with potential that when you first start looking you may have trouble seeing the trees because of the forest. Odds are, you can find an opportunity to drop an assumption or get off a premise quite soon after laying down this book. You won't have to go about looking, for as you know, problems have a knack of taking you by surprise, even though you may be so familiar with particular ones that you feel you have finally learned how to live with them. But we can accurately say that very many of them are manmade variations of one archetype: *the common assumption*. You can capitalize on the unusual situation or emergency to learn the principles of lateral thinking in order to get yourself out of the deep mental holes of "vertical thinking." Hopefully, such impromptu scenarios won't be of your own making and will be no more life threatening than the one involving this resourceful young man:

11-YEAR-OLD USES MACKEREL TO SAVE TRAPPED KITTEN

GRAND RAPIDS, Mich. (UPI)—If you want to catch a fish, you use a worm. For catching cats, an 11-year-old boy suggests a can of mackerel, which is what he used to rescue his pet kitten from a 50-foot cistern.

Raphael Bryant awoke Monday to the wails of Kit, the kitten.

After a bit of searching, Bryant and his 10-year-old brother found the cat was at the bottom of a 50-foot cistern beyond a narrow crawl space. Humane Society rescue workers couldn't lure the cat into a trap lowered into the recesses of the concrete pit. Kit also spurned a pail dropped to the bottom of the pit and a rope made of bed sheets.

Then Bryant had an idea. He fastened a long rope to a cardboard box that contained a can of mackerel, dropped his bait into the hole and, after a few minutes, retrieved his unharmed but scared pet.

Now there's a nicely symbolic example of entrapment and an unorthodox means of release that could well have been the only one possible in that particular case. The very incident can incite us to broaden our understanding of *traps, solutions, fishing,* and *bait.*

When you go assumption hunting the first place you are likely to start looking is the penny arcade of obvious prejudices and pat answers. But our biggest and most hidden biases do not pop up so easily. You might better begin your search with pat questions. The strategy here is to question your questions. As an example, suppose that your best friend has come to you for advice on how to motivate her children to put away their toys. She has tried everything—reason, reward, threats, punishment—to no sustained avail. She is at her wits end. How *can* she get her kids to put away their toys when they are through playing with them in the livingroom?

Do you have any suggestions for your friend? (Think about her dilemma for a few minutes before reading on.)

What possible solutions to the problem have you come up with? Did you remember to examine the question—How can the children be motivated to put away their playthings? Contained in the question is the assumption that your friend *needs* to motivate her kids. Maybe it would be more productive to consider ways in which the children could motivate themselves. Another assumption is that the toys *need* to be put away.[2] Is it necessary for the toys to be removed from wherever they are? Are they constituting a hazard or obstacle to other activities? If so, why not remove only those that are? If the toys are left on the livingroom floor, perhaps they will entice the children into more active play and less TV watching. Mom and Dad may even be tempted to join in the fun. The livingroom might be the ideal playroom, since many household activities (such as entertaining guests) take place in other parts of the house nowadays.

Once again we see how labels and words serve to deplete our idea stock on a deeply unconscious level. By referring to one limited area of the house as a "livingroom," we fail to see its possibilities as a playroom. Transposing such definitions to a wider context, we are able to dissolve a conflict or a difficulty before it develops into a "problem" that must be "solved." Think of the current arms build-up taking place in the United States and Russia in the name of "national security." Both countries can now destroy the world not once but fifty times over with their nuclear weaponry. Thus, "national security" has become a political euphemism that actually results in global "insecurity."

Identifying the trip wires and trap doors of conceptual assumptions is the first and foremost step in getting around, over, or under cognitive traps. In reality, however, these "traps" are nothing more than our own habitual mental circles, and getting out of them requires consistent practice in staying alert and questioning almost everything we are so used to taking for granted.

Notes

1. Edward deBono, *The Greatest Thinkers* (New York: G. P. Putnam & Sons, 1976), p. 47.
2. Arthur B. Van Gundy, *108 Ways to Get a Bright Idea* (Englewood Cliffs, N.J.: Prentice-Hall, 1983), p. 71.

Chapter Three

Subtle Influences

Conditioning is a loaded word, the sound of which does not ring pleasingly in the ear—"Who, me? Conditioned?" But everyone, without exception, is conditioned in numerous ways. This is a fact of life on earth. Many forms of psychological conditioning, unlike the physical process, are individually and socially debilitating. They veil perception and circumscribe behavior; they are the antithesis of mental expansion. Consider Webster's first entry for the verb *condition:* "To limit or modify by condition." This definition is circular, but the words *limit* and *modify* tell all. To modify means essentially to mold to fixed specifications, as to elicit a specific behavior or response in laboratory animals by manipulating stimuli.

We can also think of conditioning simply as automatic reflexes triggered by any circumstances or events in our environment, specific or general. Most natural forms of conditioning work to sustain health and life (bodily functions, language, and so on). On the other hand, many of the artificial, manmade varieties are the "fast lanes" to mental atrophy, stress, and illness. The cumulative effect of all social conditioning is mass conformity. Much of this conformity occurs outside the notoriously sleep-inducing routines of school, work place, subways, freeways, even TV. It is deeply and ceaselessly instilled through such diverse channels as cultural values (conscious and unconscious), putative religiosity, peer-group pressure, advertising in all its formats, economic need, desire for approval and attention at large, and every impulse of the ego. We do not leave conformity at the office or on the subway. George F. Babbitt (Sinclair Lewis's famous fictional character) is George F. Babbitt whether he is swinging another big real estate deal or eating breakfast. Walter Mitty (James Thurber's equally famous character) remains Walter Mitty, though he scuttles home to his alter ego after a day's role as the invisibly compliant man. Frowning or smiling, the pressure to conform is as unrelenting and consistent as the tides. It takes a strong mental swimmer to overcome the heavy currents of conformity and reach the shore of one's real self. It is a formidable challenge, which can last a lifetime. At the same time it can prove surpassingly interesting, generally enlightening, and always rewarded in the end by a greater measure of personal freedom, inner and outer.

Conditioning gets under way quite early in life, perhaps even in utero, as the evidence suggests. From the womb to the tomb our minds are molded by standardized templates for behavior, emotions, attitudes, and ultimately thought. Our beliefs, values, social status, personality, and often even individual interests are programmed right into us almost without our noticing. Very little is left in the psyche for the true individual in us to make itself known. This may explain why AI (computer) technologists are able to design computers and robots that can mimic so much human mentation and activity. Still in its infancy, this technology can already surrogate certain skills and abilities heretofore thought to be artificially unreplicable. People's jobs and in some instances entire life roles are being performed by machines. Robots can now assemble automobiles, keep files, do housekeeping chores, play Scrabble, fly airplanes, organize activities, tutor, and act as medical consults and—who knows?—may some day even be opposing each other in court. The list now "drones" on and on. These sundry feats of silicon circuitry serve to point up that, as far as our brains and our creativity are concerned, many (perhaps most?) of us are unnecessarily settling for far less than we are capable of.

Yet this negative fact can begin to open up our minds to a diametrically positive one: *We have a computer of unimaginable range and power within our own variously thick skulls; we only need to find out how to develop and activate its potentially infinite circuitry.* Sometimes we simply forget to plug it in.

Attempting to compete with high-speed computer/robots at their repetitive tasks can only result in self-defeat for the human worker. The effort will but turn the latter into inferior, stress-programmed, muscle-and-blood machines, and dehumanized humans. There is abundant evidence all around us that this process, in fact, has taken a strong hold in our culture. Lewis Yablonsky, sociologist and criminologist at California State College in Hayward, posits in his book *Robopaths*[1] that the increasing number of sociopathic cases in our society is the result of the general and rapid mechanization of people. "Robopaths," in his view, are in essence sociopaths who mindlessly conform to the powers that be. Criminal sociopaths are those who go too far with their individual pathology and violate robopathic norms and laws. The educator and writer Idries Shah sums up the machine society thus:

BEHIND THE MACHINE

Man is generally a few paces behind his own inventions.

There are still many people who are revered as figures of authority merely because they can do such things as machines can do more easily. A common example is the awe which people show when faced with someone who has only a good memory or associative capacity, often stuffed with irrelevant facts.

This recalls the refrain "man is not a machine" frequently used by people whose work and actions tend more and more to convert men into machines.

It is no accident that those cultures which most often strongly affirm the value and individuality of man are the ones which do most towards automatizing him.[2]

A buzzing example of this mass-machine mentality is the current admiration and striving emulation of Japanese production methods by the majority of Western industrialists and business experts. Floods of books and articles on theory Z and other cost-efficient techniques have found their way into the hands and heads of corporate managers. American and European manufacturers are hiring Japanese consultants to train their own production heads. A number of Japanese techniques can certainly be adopted elsewhere, but the wholesale import of these ideas into societies that have not developed, as the Japanese have, safeguards against the dangers of mass mechanization (preservation of traditional arts, customs, social cohesion, religion, and the like), may perpetuate, as Yablonsky predicts, trends of depersonalization, alienation, and brutality.

The preceding observations are in no way meant to portray artificial intelligence as a technological *bête noire* threatening human supremacy. Nor are we suggesting that anyone who switches on a computer automatically switches off his or her brain. Some workers in this field are in fact more humanistically creative than, say, many of those in nontech professions, such as the social services. Nonetheless, certain experts in AI see clear dangers for human society and individual volition in our mass preoccupation with the computer. Joseph Weizenbaum at MIT believes that these digital wunderkinds focus thought quite subtly from multidimensionality into unidimensionality, as required by the concretized vocabulary and sequential operations of their programs. That computers are indeed enticing diversions, touted as fun and games by those with vested interests in them, tends to conceal their thought-narrowing effects.

Thomas Keenan, associate professor of computer science at the University of Calgary, Alberta, Canada, thinks that more and more individuals will seek emotional fulfillment in computers instead of in other people as the former are increasingly refined to interact with and imitate humans, especially vocally. Which gives "pushes my button" and "turns me on" new dimensions of expression. So it is not inconceivable that in the future one AI program could be handling your finances by day while another breaks out the champagne or consoles you in your bankruptcy at night.

But we can't blame the machines for being themselves—perhaps in the future we will need all the friends we can get, flesh or "firmware." We can fault the robotoid inclinations of their human advocates, who often do not see their possible negative impacts as clearly as the creators themselves. What is it in "human nature" that is so fond of the robot? What is the origin of all this liking for things automated? For a shade of an answer, we will take a further look at the substance of conditioning.

Pavlov discovered in the early 1900s that salivation in dogs could be triggered by a simple ringing bell and nothing more. At first the dogs were subjected to consecutive soundings of the bell just before feeding time. After a time on this program, the dogs would continue to salivate at the bell even though their food was repeatedly withheld. Hungry or not, they would drool whenever the bell sounded. Gradually, though, this effect would diminish, the conditioned reflex at last "extinguished." Thus *Pavlovian conditioning*.

In contrast, *operant conditioning* refers to a more engineered kind of behavior whereby the organism (animal or man) must take a specific action (or "operate") on its environment in order to obtain reward or avoid punishment. A monkey, for example, learns to press a series of levers to receive food—trial-and-error learning.

Although these two rudimentary modes of conditioning do occur outside of laboratories, most human and social phenomena is much, much more subtle and pervasive. How much does our conditioned acquisitiveness salivate at the sight or thought of the nice things in the shops? How many consumer levers do we push daily in hope of getting those nice things? Strengthening this bell ringing of desires is the instillation of mutually reinforcing opinions, beliefs, values, and attitudes. This complex might be described as cognitive conditioning or indoctrination. The frailties of gullibility and suggestibility as well as the various carrot sticks of conformity render the human mind a ready receptacle for indoctrination. This level of mental molding occurs outside of awareness most of the time for the reason that it circumfuses us so completely, like psychic pollution; we constantly partake of it while thinking of it hardly at all. Therefore we should not be surprised at recent studies demonstrating that what consciousness we are capable of is in fact on French leave much more often than we want to admit.

If we credit the proposition of our frequently AWOL minds, then we must also consider that what we are pleased to call our beliefs, preferences and ideas might not be the product of our individual consciousness and so not really ours after all. A century of sociological and psychological studies shows us that personal autonomy is closer to idealistic fiction than fact, even in modern "democratic" societies, and that culture itself is the implanter of lifetime mental sets, via a comprehensive seeding of norms, mores (traditions, customs), values, and priorities. To repeat, the bulk of this implanting takes place on subconscious levels, both verbally and nonverbally.

With the advent of mass communications in modern society, mind and behavior shaping reached into the private sanctum of the home. Conditioning moved right in with television and replaced the vacuum-tube radio with the video screen. The mind-soothing warmth of the flickering hearth was pushed into nostalgia by the strident vibrations of electronic media. The slogan of the pioneering media analyst Marshall McLuhan, "The medium is the message" (also the title of one of his books), sums up the mind-channeling power of electronic attendance. His work defined the powerful dynamics and effects of the communications technologies in modern life, while other critics, such as Vance Packard (*The People Shapers, The Hidden Persuaders*),[3] zeroed in on the media's stimulation of consumer appetites and manipulation of public perceptions for political and profit-making ends.

Evidence of mass brain-blinkering piles up rather quickly when it is given voice and vote in opinion surveys. Results of two polls undeniably link up media exposure with popularity, ego status, declining humanitarianism, and perhaps more than a jot of political nihilism.

In a Gallup youth survey taken in December 1982 a representative national cross section of 500 young men and women, ages thirteen through eighteen, were asked: "What man you have heard or read about and who is alive today in any part of the world do you admire most—not including any of your relatives or friends? Who is your second choice?" The results:

- President Reagan
- Pope John Paul II
- Former President Carter
- Prince Charles
- Barney Clark
- Senator Edward Kennedy
- Burt Reynolds
- Menachem Begin
- Jerry Lewis
- "Sugar Ray" Leonard

An interesting mix, don't you think? Although it is hard to imagine all these fellows rollicking together in the same frat house, they all had one thing in common: loads of airtime. (Barney Clark, now deceased, was the first recipient of the artificial heart.) Otherwise this was quite a jumble of stardom (image) and substance, both of which, many will agree, are distortions in some of the choices. Such ratings correlate to the amount of publicity personalities and events generate, more than to any other factor. In fact, that was a conclusion of the poll itself; ratings were *directly proportionate* to the amount of publicity received. And an even more revealing finding was that the teenagers polled *thought* they were *expected* to respond as to who is *admired* and were not to make their choices solely on their judgment of these individual's achievements. Such is the seduction of power and image.

This sort of unreflective, ready-made response is a perfect illustration of media mind programming, indoctrination in its rosiest disguise. The indoctrinated mind fails to think for itself. It has been trained not to by programs of indoctrination that are not recognized as such. Ergo, we can say that very few of us understand what indoctrination really is and relate brain-washing only to sordid scenes of torture under interrogation lamps in B movies, a favorite indoor sport of Nazis and Commies. Closer to home, such surveys as those cited above as well as diverse psychological studies shed some uncomfortably glaring light on the less savory aspects of conditioning in our own society. Naturally it would be erroneous to try to paint a full portrait of the national psyche from such research, but disturbing elements do emerge in the developing profile.

In another poll, conducted in February 1983 by the University of Massachusetts, 792 (out of 2000) representative male and female Americans, when asked whether they would rather be "dead than Red," answered yes. That is, they would rather fight an all-out nuclear war than live under Communist rule, *even if the bombs killed everyone in the United States.* Russophobia aside, it would be interesting to know to what extent paranoia pervades American life at more personal levels. Paranoia seems to be a sort of psychic toxin that seeps into the vacuums of mindlessness. As Padraig O'Malley, senior analyst at the university's Center for Policy Studies notes, the results reflected a basic deficiency in understanding the scope of nuclear holocaust and an "ingrained" notion (with all that implies) of life under communism. O'Malley attributes this knee-jerk "better dead than Red" response of one-third of the pollees to the heavy hand of politicization. Selective perception and dogmatic denial of incriminating evidence increasingly mark the modern political scene. Not to mention the deliberate obscuring and minimizing of unflattering facts. As remarkable as the findings of the U. of Massachusetts survey were, it was curiously given but a brief, inconspicuous coverage on the back page of the *Phoenix Gazette* (April 6, 1983), a newspaper long known for its right-wing sentiments.

If today's youth were actually educated to think, rather than trained to parrot "correct" answers to the fixed questions of a cracker (grade) giver, their admiration might be directed to other personages than the media-hyped favored in the Gallup poll. Some admiration is warranted (depending on your persuasions) on the list, but note that no Nobel Prize winners are on it, nor are any scientists, thinkers, writers, or inventors. Macho and glamor are there in abundance, as is authority and political power. Magnanimity and its absence both claim places on the list but are probably heavily colored by bias-tinted PR lenses.

The rallying cry of 1960s youth was "Question authority." The cry seemed to lose its very breath through the seventies, and today in the early eighties it can be heard only as a plaintive whine here and there. When a slogan is not supported by follow-through, it remains only a slogan and runs out of energy before long. Then too little is left for the acid test. The problem is we often don't know how, where, and when to question authority. Consider the work of social scientist Stanley Milgram, who documented the "shocking" results of his studies of "obedience to authority," in a book of the same name.[4]

In extensive research involving about 300,000 people and using the same basic experimental design, Milgram discovered, much to his and everyone else's surprise, that under pressure from authority 85 percent of all subjects tested would knowingly inflict pain on others. The paradigm experiment was conducted under the guise of a study to find out how effective punishment was in facilitating learning (i.e., memory tasks); the volunteer "teachers" being ignorant of the true purpose of the experiment. The mock "learners" were supposedly hooked up to electrodes, while the subject-teachers, walled off from the learners, were instructed to shock them by turning a knob on a console each time the learners responded incorrectly to a question. Each time a learner (Milgram's confederate) made an error, a trainer was urged by the experimenter himself, who was recording everything, to increase the voltage. The confederate actor-learner had been coached beforehand to match the imaginary increase in voltage with a correspondingly louder vocal response. With experimenters at their elbows and egging them on, twenty-five out of forty people obeyed to the very end of the test, finally administering the would-be lethal 450 volt shocks. This average held throughout hundreds of precisely duplicated experiments.

Milgram's bold undertaking turned out to be quite an ethical shock to nearly everyone who took an interest in it. Typically, most people on hearing about it identify with the 15 percent of the pain-inflictors who did not "top out" in scary obedience. But this too is illusory, since the 85 percent obedience factor is even higher than the findings suggest. The 15 percent who refused to cooperate did so in a relatively "obedient" manner; they made no move to help the learner, complain to higher authorities, or rebuke the experimenter. Instead, they kept their assigned places at all times, excused themselves apologetically and mildly awaited dismissal by the *authority in charge*. What would these dutiful decliners have done if they had been told they themselves would be punished for refusing to obey?

In follow-up interviews, Milgram discovered that embarrassment at wavering in their duty, a strong desire to keep their promise to help the researchers, and a deeply ingrained sense of politeness all added up cooperation to a large fault. Such is the stuff of conditioning.

But now that we know something more about the negative effects of conditioning, what can we do about it? The answer is, not a great deal straight away, but perhaps much more than you might expect over the remainder of your life, providing that you are willing and have the ability to study its dynamics in yourself and society and to make sustained, propitious efforts to neutralize it where and when it is counterproductive. Conditioning, after all, has been narrowing us all down from day one; it is unrealistic to expect to unshackle ourselves from it without long-term strategy and work. The most expeditious first step we can take is to realize our situation as that of a would-be escapee who possesses few or no escape skills, nor fully understands the required conditions for the escape itself. Not to absorb these preliminary facts is to fail to begin. (Impressive advances in drug development and electronic control of brain function via surgically implanted electrodes and transmitters are apt to give one the mistaken notion that actual "mind control" can take place only by use of such physical methods. In reality, however, these techniques are seldom necessary for behavioral manipulation, in either totalitarian or democratic societies, since conformity for nearly everyone is achieved quite early in childhood by the "soft" methods discussed in this chapter.)

Fortunately, useful suggestions and information can be offered to those who are prepared to begin study of counterconditioning principles. It is important to remember that there are no verbal, sure-fire formulas for this effort, particularly of the timetable variety. On the contrary, tight mental sets are part and parcel of the complex that leads to inflexibility of thought, a precondition, as it were, to the permanent ossification of the mind/brain. Mental sets merely spin the cognitive wheels deeper into the ruts of conditioning, though they may give the sensation of forward movement.

In his excellent guidebook *The Observing Self: Mysticism and Psychotherapy*, Arthur J. Deikman, M.D., devotes a chapter to defining "the trance of ordinary life." He clearly outlines the similarity between clinical hypnotic induction and the fixated preoccupations of everyday life. Because the latter does not involve cushy furnishings and soft suggestions, we may not make the connections. Yet, as Deikman points out, the conditions of trance are present on the street outside of the hypnotist's office: restricted awareness, fixed attention, automatized behavior, and ongoing fantasy states. Deikman describes the therapeutic tools and techniques that can help wake us from this "sleep" into a more healthy reality freer of obsessions and compulsions, one such approach being to endeavor to free oneself "from the biases and assumptions of the culture."[6]

Behavior therapy is undoubtedly the most popular treatment for changing or neutralizing specific, undesired habits. The techniques used include hypnosis (and self-hypnosis), desensitization and other deconditioning methods, and thought control. All of these must first target the conditioned problem behavior and then counter it with some tactic designed to extinguish it. Usually these strategies focus upon symptoms believed to be learned: phobias and fears, obsessions, and compulsive responses to particular stimuli. For example, a phobia for flying in airplanes might be worked on with a combination of relaxation and positive imagery, the word *airplane* associated with clouds and drowsiness. At a certain stage, pictures of airplanes may be presented to the patient and perhaps supervised visits to airports made to complete familiarization with the actual environment.

The effectiveness of behavior therapies vary from low to high, depending on the intensity of the problem, the idiosyncrasies of the patient, and the abilities of the therapist. One problem with these approaches is that they are too simplistic and treat effects rather than causes. The assumption that all symptoms are learned is highly questionable. It could well be instead that in many cases the symptom(s) develops out of a large complex of environmental, genetic, and circumstantial factors not currently identified. Protracted experiences entailing pain, conflict, frustration, and the like cannot be reduced to simple stimulus/response formulae. Many situations are probably much more intricate than the behavioral clinicians suspect.

A related complication of behavior therapies, which frequently militates against their restoration of overall emotional health in patients' lives, is the almost totally unrecognized one of habit displacement. This is somewhat like removing a rotten apple in a pile; you may indeed get the undesirable one out but bring down the whole structure in the process. Or perhaps there are many other rotten ones concealed inside. So treating symptoms instead of syndromes and the broader pathology can be very risky business, especially when attempted by an inexperienced or inept therapist. Sometimes the problem is made worse.

Thus while the adoption of behavior modification principles to certain discrete problems associated with conditioning may have some secondary effectiveness, it is much less likely to be successful in reversing the mind-diminishing processes of mass social conditioning and even less so in psychoprophylaxis (prevention). These methodologies by themselves do not develop a balanced perspective on life, one that prevents habit and conformity from warping one's mental propensities into biased, closed patterns.

Writer Denise Winn makes a superb analysis of conditioning phenomena in her book *The Manipulated Mind*. In the chapter "Resisting Influence" Winn offers several strategies, proven under extreme conditions, that serve to sustain one's sense of reality through correct perception in times of stress and/or duress. One of these is humor, the capacity for which frequently decreases in people as the going gets tougher. But as Winn points out, maintaining the ability to laugh at whoever or whatever would coerce or manipulate renders the oppressor impotent to ultimately control and exploit the laughter. Such was the case of Turkish prisoners of war in the Korean conflict. When their Chinese interrogators accused them of war crimes, the Turks would robustly deride the suggestion, make jokes about their accusers' information sources, and implicitly question their intelligence. The Chinese were at a loss, their technique of guilt inducement down an unexpected drain. That's the wonderful twist of a good joke; it blows stifling expectations out of the mind and lets in good air.

Another method Winn advises in resisting conditioning is simple emotional detachment. When we are too wrapped up in ourselves, our surroundings, or other people, we are mental putty in the hands of others. Our world easily becomes nothing more than a set of obsessive thoughts binding us to an authority figure(s). However, by "standing back, emotionally, and testing our assumptions," says Winn, we are better able to "become more the masters of ourselves and correspondingly less the slaves of circumstance."[7] Indeed, this practice has proven its efficacy in the most adverse and prolonged kinds of circumstances, as in concentration camps and political prisons.

Although defenses such as humor and detachment can be consciously honed to get oneself through any kind of trying situation, they should be naturally integrated into a larger framework of self-knowledge and understanding of the general "human condition." Any way of gaining insight is eminently valuable in this respect. Beyond this there are well-established paths to enlightenment such as the esoteric Eastern schools of Zen, Yoga, and Sufism. These traditions claim to possess developmental means of bypassing conditioning and connecting the mind to greater reality outside of false social influences. Yet there are many bogus schools that make this assertion also, advertising themselves under the same name as the genuine one. Should we encounter an authentic school, we should find the essence of deconditioning itself.

In the following chapters many of the foregoing observations on conditioning will at times be elaborated on and further clarified. Readers are invited to make as many of their own connections as they can.

Notes

1. Lewis Yablonsky, *Robopaths* (New York: Bobbs-Merrill, 1972).
2. Idries Shah, *Reflections* (Baltimore: Penguin Books, 1972), p. 77.
3. Vance Packard, *The People Shapers* (Boston: Little, Brown, 1977).
4. Vance Packard, *The Hidden Persuaders* (New York: Pocket Books, 1957).
5. Stanley Milgram, *Obedience To Authority* (New York: Harper & Row, 1973).
6. Arthur J. Deikman, *The Observing Self: Mysticism and Psychotherapy* (Boston: Beacon Press, 1982), p. 130.
7. Denise Winn, *The Manipulated Mind* (London: Octagon Press, 1983), p. 212.

Chapter Four

Blindside

There was once a small, remote archipelago, which, for the events to be described, we will call Myopia. The human population on each of the three islands forming this short chain was isolated from the rest of the world and semi-isolated from its neighbor islands, owing more to mental barriers than to distance itself.

The inhabitants of Myopia displayed the general range of human traits and propensities we observe everywhere today. The several Myopian cultures reflected these, some developments being expansive and eclectic, all too many being insular and retrograde. During one period a particular cult, custom, or technical innovation might be sanctioned by the rulers, at other times it might be *de trop*. Now this clan or creed might hold sway over the people, now that one. The pattern is familiar.

A fateful occurrence took place during an otherwise typical cycle of Myopia's tri-culture, setting off a chain of events that was to hasten the end of island life as it had existed prior to this event.

One placid afternoon a stately sailing ship ventured into an inlet of the outermost (from the mainland) island and dropped anchor. A score of natives were then gathering shells on the beach. From time to time they would look up and gaze in the vessel's direction, yet never seeming to register its presence.

A boat was lowered from the ship and men descended into it and rowed toward the shore and the beachcombers. And still the latter did not see the visitors. As the rowboat neared, however, a vague agitation began welling up in the shell hunters and they chattered and squinted seaward ever more anxiously. Still no one pointed out the alien presence or sounded an alarm. As the boat careened over the foaming breakers, the natives stood transfixed, as witnesses to a stark apparition, at last backing away. When the boatmen tumbled into the surf with hearty greetings, the primitives about-faced and raced up into the forested mountains of the interior to their village as fast as their legs would carry them.

Upon receiving the terrifying news of the landing of the strange beings, the shaman-chief of the island immediately ordered a great gathering of all the people for mass supplication to their major deity, the Spirit of the Rock. This was a boulder balanced none too permanently atop a small foothill. Within hours nearly every islander had assembled at the ceremonial site to beseech the Boulder-Spirit for deliverence from the "sea demons." But soon after the chief began his incantations, hysteria overcame the entire throng, and they pressed so heavily upon the boulder that it became dislodged, toppling off its perch and crushing a large number of people, including the chief and all of the huddled elders of the tribe.

Chaos swept over the island like a flood tide, destroying the very fabric of island society. Like the boulder, life itself was hurtled with an unstoppable momentum into the lowest depths; compassion and cooperation were rapidly displaced by ruthless competition for sustenance and dominance. This anarchy reigned until a new kind of order was restored, which is beyond the scope of our story.

After a few days of exploring and coast charting, the ship's crew reboarded, weighed anchor, and set sail for the next island. Some fishermen were casting their nets offshore when the ship appeared on the horizon and slowed to its moorings. Taking belated notice of it, the fishermen fell into argument whether it was the legendary Great Gull—and therefore the best of omens—or the Ghost Cloud, a dreadful portent that signaled many months of poor fishing and resultant famine.

The dispute ended abruptly when the sails of the craft came down. To the observers this baffling turn of events meant something even more negative and ominous than a coming scarcity of fish, though they did not know what it did signify. Being of highly emotional stock, these fishermen and their people were not inclined to reason about the phenomenon. Indeed, almost overnight the entire populace entered a deep thrombosis that prevented them from going near the sea, much less fishing in it. But since fish had been their staple food and only source of protein, soon malnourishment, disease, and mental impairment deteriorated every quarter of the society. Little did anyone realize that their troubles were caused by neither gull nor cloud but rather by fear itself, which was self-fulfilling.

A much healthier state of affairs existed on the third and last island when the voyagers arrived, at least materially. Abundance had long since made life a constant sensual dream in the balmy clime. The natives filled up all of their leisure time with eating, sex, sporting contests, and various other diversions. Their religion amounted to little more than a ceremonial sanctioning of this lifestyle, although it took on the face of utmost gravity and ritual decorum. The handful of spirits (depicted on carved totems) were deified as the protectors of the panoply of collective indulgences. Some idea of an afterlife had germinated in the totem worship, however it was conceived of in most minds as but an intensification of earthly pleasures.

Now an outstanding characteristic of these people was a highly developed sense of social propriety and protocol. Correctness (as defined by custom) of dress, makeup, and behavior was paramountly important. In fact, it might be said that appearance became almost everything the moment an islander stepped out of his dwelling.

So, the strangers from the "big canoe" were received by the chief and his entourage with unprecedented pomp and ceremony. The latter had made tenuous contact with seafarers before, with generally pleasant effects, and had no delusions about their being spirits or "signs."

Nonetheless, the guests were made much over, their clothing and accoutrements being the objects of no end of ah-ing and oh-ing. Focused so intently on these trappings, the islanders did not notice the frequent glaze of greed and treachery that possessed the eyes of some of the visitors. And they assumed that the muskets they carried must be symbols of status and/or magical talismans. As the two groups communicated mainly by hand gestures, questions concerning such things could not be effectively asked, or much pertinent information exchanged.

It happened that the chief had recently been plagued with chronic migraine headaches. He wondered if the captain of the ship might be able to drive the evil out of his skull with the help of the wondrously crafted instrument that seldom left his shoulder. This idea the chief succeeded in conveying to the captain via hand motions. "No, it cannot be done," the captain waved back his answer. The chief interpreted this response as one of simple refusal, instead of the statement of impossibility which it was. He was affronted, although maintaining his polite composure, and the meeting broke up with an acute tension that was yet far from hostility.

Several of the captain's crew, however, had seen a possibility in the situation, centering around the jewels that adorned the chief's body. A plot was hatched.

That night one of the schemers stole up to the chief's hut, called him out and proffered his firearm to him in the moonlight. But first he demonstrated to the chief how it was to be operated as a cure for headache. In return he asked for and received the precious gem necklace the chief had worn the night before. Then the plotters ducked into the bush and listened for the gunshot, which was not long in coming.

What then followed is for the reader to image.

If you think the preceding story is all fiction, think again. When Magellan's expedition first landed at Tierra del Fuego, the Fuegan natives, who used canoes and who had for centuries been isolated from the rest of the world, were unable to see the ship anchored in the bay. The remainder of the tale is more truth than imagination as well, based as it is on the documented kind of behavior insulated people typically display when faced with concrete phenomena that cannot be fitted into their culturally constructed reality—i.e., their belief system. Modern, technologized people display this behavior as much as primitves do.

Such amazing examples of denial constitute almost archetypal evidence for a historically widespread blindness in the human brain, manifesting in specific groups of people (nations, creeds, associations, and so on) as what might be called assumptive astigmatism. This perceptual malady is no less prevalent in modern, technological societies than in remote, primitive cultures, albeit in the former it is unconsciously rationalized and concealed in layers of mislaid logic. The UFO and similar controversies are in large part rendered meaningless by so much conflicting "eyewitness" testimony, for it has been shown in case after case that observation and recall are so often distorted in firsthand reports that the independent descriptions of two or more witnesses seem frequently to almost be of different events. Add to this the recorded evidence of individual and mass hallucination (the flip side of the Fuegan experience), and the complications of what is today known as tunnel vision begin to appear formidable.

In his penetrating book *Total Man*, Stan Gooch makes a case for psychosis as a "literal reality" for contemporary man. He claims, in a chapter called "The Psychotic Society," that this aberration is so common, so embedded in our social fabric, that we cannot see even its most manifest absurdities.[1] Cultural conditioning gathers a perceptual fog around the individual's senses, blinding him or her to things as they really are. Such consensual unreality is often quite obvious to an alien or someone outside of the mainstream culture. Many unfamiliar customs of non-Western peoples are viewed as repulsive barbarisms by Americans and Europeans, while numerous unhealthy and unnatural ones of their own are rarely questioned by them.

Thus cannibalism and suttee (in which a Hindu widow sacrifices herself upon her husband's funeral pyre) were looked upon in horror by white missionaires, all the while the soldiers behind them were slaying natives in the name of God. Once established, the missionaries maintained power by practicing psychic cannibalism on the people and leaving their spirit in ashes, when not their villages. And today, no less than in colonial times, various tribal practices such as lip-stretching and wearing bones in the nose for one version of attractiveness are considered bizarre by Westerners, yet our own habits of dangling rings from the ears (and sometimes piercing them), plucking the eyebrows, shaving the face, doing all manner of things to the hair of the head, getting "nose jobs" and face-lifts are taken as normal pursuits of beauty.

Likewise, our obsession with hygiene often seems outlandish to foreigners and contradictory as well when they become aware of the pollution and contamination of our larger environment. Several more of the "symptoms" of psychosis Gooch indexes are technologized warfare; killing at a distance, without the killers' ever seeing or knowing the victims (bombing, napalming, germ warfare); and high-rise, file-cabinet-style architecture of nonorganic construction, which blocks both the view and natural air circulation and often dispenses with fire escapes. The windows in high-rise office buildings do not open, and the people inside are totally dependent on artificial air from air conditioning systems and heat pumps. Artificial air is charged with positive ions, which have been shown to cause respiratory ailments (allergies, proneness to flu viruses, and so on) and depression, owing to fluctuation of the brain hormone serotonin. Gooch's list goes on for pages and constitutes an impressive case for institutionalized insanity in our society, although there are various healthy countertrends.

But individual or mass, the syndrome of cerebral blindness does not occur full-blown overnight or even over a few years. It seems to be precursed by certain seemingly innocuous tendencies toward delusion and illusion. It is beyond the scope of this book to explicate these processes in depth, though we can define the complex of delusion, illusion, and blindness as a subjective state, legitimitized by conformity. Falling in line with rank-and-file standards of behavior and appearance has become a total way of life for the majority of people, at least affording a degree of anonymous security if not overt approval. Most people in any given society are conformists, no matter how hard they might object. Think of the endless scores of behavioral no-nos in our own "free" society, which although they are but peccadillos, may still result in the social ostracism of the individuals who persist in practicing them. In the United States many such taboos are markedly gendered.

Have you ever seen a woman smoke a pipe? A few—a very few—may fire up a stogie now and then, but almost never a pipe. Why not? Millions of men puff and enjoy pipes daily—why should the pleasure be denied women? Perhaps the possibility is culturally premature; after all, women didn't get the cigarette without public hassle until several decades after men. And finally, in our time, pants. It is safe to say that today, for casual wear, trousers are more common than skirts and dresses on women. Yet other than Scotsmen on parade, have you ever known or heard of a man strutting his macho in a skirt? Men cross-dressers are still pretty much in the closet, while women have made great strides in this direction. No doubt we are wading into murky social waters here, since the whole subject of dress is so suffused with sexual content—repression, fetishism, "sex-role confusion," homosexuality—that to consider it in nonsexual terms is nigh onto impossible, owing to conditioning at a very deep level. Not to mention the greater world of behavior. We leave it to you: Can a man wear a skirt, a woman smoke a pipe, and still remain all man or all woman? Where does reality leave off and bias begin?

To grasp the deeper and broader nature of cerebral blindsidedness, it is helpful to examine it within the context of time. As we all know, fashions, trends, and attitudes rise and fall as regularly as the tides—ergo, the ups and downs of skirt hemlines. This cyclical character of the social psyche is a feature of what has been generally referred to as Zeitgeist, or time spirit. Webster defines it loosely as "the spirit of the age; trend of thought and feeling in a period." It is a sort of collective mentality, conceptual conformity encompassing a given culture at a given moment in historical time. The Zeitgeists of the various cultures worldwide together make up the fabric of global consciousness, which might well resemble a psychic crazy-quilt to an extraterrestrial visitor. We can think of our own Zeitgeist as a locally peculiar mental atmosphere, one much more influential than any weather pattern.

The best insight into the Zeitgeist phenomenon is afforded by our present technological era and its depersonalizing effects on every spectrum of human interaction. One of many vivid illustrations of this is the interesting history of child rearing, as traced by Daniel Beekman in his thorough book, *The Mechanical Baby*. By spanning over half a millenium of bringing up Junior, Beekman reveals how each generation has viewed and practiced child rearing, in turn reflecting the dominating social philosophy of the period.[2] In the early twentieth century, with the industrial age well under way, parents were led to believe that their offspring could be tooled to perfection. Gone was the Victorian model of "correct child," purged of his "natural evil" by moralistic "spare the rod and spoil the child" rationale. *Regularity* rather than *discipline* became the buzz word. Beekman cites a poem, "For the Young Mother" (circa 1921), composed by Myrtle Eldren and Helen LeCron, which sums up the credo of the era:

> *The clock is the Baby's truest friend*
> *As every Mother ought to know!*
>
> *From early dawn to evening's end,*
> *It points the way the day should go!*
>
> *"Wake up!" it says at six o'clock,*
> *"Wake up and have your morning meal!"*
>
> *And later, "Time to bathe, (tick, tock!)"*
> *And "Oh, how happy you will feel!"*
>
> *Then, "Eat again," then, "Sleep," then "Take*
> *Your daily airing," thus it goes—*
>
> *So mother ought, for Baby's sake,*
> *To take the clock's advice! It knows!*[3]

Thenceforth scientific technology insinuated itself into the family household as, among other things, Nanny. "If technology could guarantee consistency in manufactured goods," Beekman cites the reasoning, "why couldn't it also guarantee the production of consistently wonderful children?" Scheduling and precision were the keystones of success in engineering a better Junior. The child-rearing manual of those halcyon years of Henry Ford was Dr. Luther Emmet Holt's *The Care and Feeding of Children*.[4] In it, strict dietary formulas are prescribed, down to the exact number of ounces of milk, sugar, lime water, boiled water, and barley gruel, "these figures to be varied exactly as recommended, ounce by ounce, every two weeks as the baby grows." In response to other uncertainties, such as, "How much crying is normal for a very young baby?" Holt responds true to form: "From fifteen to thirty minutes a day is not too much." He further advises the use of mechanical contraptions such as thigh spreaders (to prevent chafing) and aluminum mittens (to stop thumb sucking).

Beekman continues his etiology of child care through the "common-sense" years of Dr. Spock with its emphasis on permissiveness, right up to the present time of ultrapsychologistic strategies for producing the "ideal child." The updated model of Jack and Jill perfection seems to have been drawn up on Mt. Olympus: "healthy, happy, energetic, intelligent, and a friendly extrovert." The failure to nurture such a Superior Being often results in parents' feeling like dismal underachievers in the great child-show competition. Because of the pressures of conformity, few dare to challenge or opt out of the "mechanical baby" paradigm.

The child-rearing philosophy sketched above was dealt with at some length in the interest of showing the immense powers of Zeitgeist—"time spirit"—and the insidious forces of imitation, subjectivity, and conformity that historically accompany it. It is these conditions that make for social myopia, the bane of true progress under the guise of "progressiveness." The Zeitgeist itself is a dynamically neutral process, neither positive nor negative, as is time itself.

Yet when all is said and done, mass blindness is but a negative magnification of individual unperceptiveness. Overemotionalism and rationalization usually go together to make up the personal pair of blinkers most of us wear. Looking for a lost object is a notoriously common example of this effect. Often the missing article is under our very nose, and someone else points it out to us. Until it is found, however, we may get in a dudgeon, accuse others of mislaying it, and imagine a dozen scenarios of what could have happened to it. More often than not our very pronouncements are more self-descriptive than we know: "I'm so mad I can't see straight," and "I don't *see* it that way."

Becoming more perceptually objective means developing a modicum of inner control, as contrasted to the sense-shrinking effects of external conditioning (social regulation, coercion, and so on). This personal autonomy should not be confused with self-censuring and repression—which are at bottom culturally instilled—but understood as the cultivation of nonattachment. As Gautama Buddha stressed, attachment is the root cause of all human misery.

Nonattachment, or detachment, is simply the mental practice of getting *outside* of any situation, however personal or prevalent such a situation may be. It is not, as frequently posited, the equivalent of noninvolvement; it may or may not require involvement. But its essence is *nonidentifying* with a particular point of view (which is usually our own). The practitioner of detachment may come to support a point of view that he or she sees as more valid than another, but the practitioner begins with a dispassionate overview.

Real detachment does not effectively demand the physical austerities of monks and yogis in monasteries or postured meditation. However, a practiced quietude of mind is necessary for getting free of the immediate obsessions and compulsions that distort one's perceptual processes and behavior.

Actually there are scores of ways, active and passive, to gear down your brain in order to take in more of the panorama of reality and gain extra perspective on yourself and your world. The following are only a few of the many possibilities.

- Reflect periodically that your world is but one in an infinite multitude, material and immaterial, from vast to infinitesimal. Although your world is primarily important to you, remember that your personal sphere of existence and concern may be quite different from that of another being, even another human. Reading expansive, nonspecialized books and articles on astronomy, cosmology, physics, and metaphysics is an excellent way of enlarging your mental world and taking hold of more reality in its dimensional aspects.

- Recall some of your past judgments, hopes, fears, and imaginings that turned out to be groundless, the very stuff of uncreative, perception-clouding subjectivity. Diaries, picture albums, yearbooks, and so on, may help generate or cast more light on the memories of these. Remember that year you or someone you knew was so sure that the United States and Russia would be at war within days? How about when those new neighbors seemed so weird to you when you watched them moving in, though they turned out to be interesting and decent folk once you got to know them?

- Define for yourself the meaning of *strange* in the context of human behavior. Then make an honest, diligent effort to understand how what is most familiar to you might seem strange or alien to a foreigner, or vice versa. Write down the things you like least and most about the society you live in and what might seem strange or normal about them as seen in the eyes of someone from another culture or time. Start with what is closest to you (social interactions, customs, dress, environmental conditions).

Probably one of the biggest steps you can take in overcoming perceptual shortsightedness is to endeavor to *see yourself as others see you*. That is easier said than done, however. Above all, it requires a great deal of self-honesty. It also requires humility. The object is to see yourself through the eyes of others—not as you would like to *believe* they see you. Work on it. Besides allowing you to come to terms with your own subjectivity, this is an "exercise" that forces you to get more from your brain.

Notes

1. Stan Gooch, *Total Man* (New York: Ballantine Books, 1972).
2. Daniel Beekman, *The Mechanical Baby* (New York: New American Library, 1977).

3. Ibid., p. 109. The poem originally appeared in Eldred Mrs. Myrtle and LeCron, Helen C. *For the Young Mother*. Chicago: Reilly & Lee, 1921.
4. Luther Emmet Holt, *The Care and Feeding of Children* (New York: Appleton, 1903).

Chapter Five

Attention Factor

One of Sal's sons returned home on leave from the army. Over postprandial whiskey and cigars, Sal asked him confidentially how he really like the military service.

"Not that much, Dad," the lad confided. "The army is stripping me of my individuality."

"Those damned thieves," exclaimed Sal; "don't let them get away with it!" And then quietly: "Son, you're not trying to wear it *all* on the outside of your uniform, are you?"

We could no more live in society without attention than we could, say, cross a busy street without being seen. Living things require increasing attendance and sustenance as they ascend the evolutionary ladder, and even our inanimate possessions need some upkeep. A house plant must be watered, placed in proper light, perhaps trimmed. A female sea turtle abandons her eggs only after burying them in the right location and depth of sand. Laboratory monkeys become sickly and neurotic in isolation, even when their diet and hygiene are good.

As a human need, however, the plot of attention thickens, for in the arenas of recognition, publicity, image projection, behavior manipulation, and the like, attention becomes as much a narcotic as a nutrient, as harmful to the individual and society as any hard drug. Quite unfortunately this phenomenon is not widely realized. On the contrary, the "more is better" consumer impulse prevails, and the result is that attention is indeed a socially synthesized and sanctioned stimulant on which some people are literally overdosing, whereas others do not receive enough to maintain their psychophysical health.

It has been only in the last twenty years that psychology has paid much attention to attention. Interest in its physiology was furthered by the discovery of the ascending reticular activating system (ARAS), a portion of the brain stem associated with sleep and arousal. About the same time, during studies of animal conditioning, physiological psychologists also identified an "attention reflex," technically dubbed the orienting reflex (OR). Like the knee-jerk reflex, it is a semiautomatic reaction to a new stimulus or environmental change. Once adapted to the stimulus (e.g., after several repetitions), the organism no longer exhibits the OR and is deemed to be in a state of habituation.

Aside from these few external indicators, modern psychology has found out very little about attention as a vital factor in human learning and behavior. Idries Shah, in *Learning How to Learn*, brings this to light in a section entitled "On Attention." He stresses the largely hidden aspects of attention as a human need and suggests that its study would be best pursued by first identifying its phases of attraction, extension, reception, and interchange in various social activities. He then makes twenty-one original observations on attention dynamics, each one of practical value.[1] For our present purpose we need only focus on several general effects.

An initially important point made by Shah is that many human interactions, including those considered to be serious and high-minded, are actually "disguised attention-situations." That is a loaded assessment but nonetheless one worthy of much reflection. One implication is that the misuse of attention may—and probably does—lead to much social and individual deception, inefficiency, and misunderstanding.

As with most of the other principles discussed in this book, the processes involved in this one are not given to simplification. On the other hand, you can study them under your very nose, so to speak. The advantage in sensitizing yourself to the workings of attention in your daily life is that you will be more attuned to true motives (both yours and others) as opposed to the implied motives in various situations. Hence you can become more realistic in your perceptions and proficient in your undertakings.

Suppose, for instance, that you are a not unattractive woman who has lately been the object of continuing sexual innuendos from a male coworker in your office. Satisfied that you are not unwittingly cueing this Lothario, how best to discourage him?

To ward off this kind of unsolicited attention without creating an unnecessarily nasty scene or bad feelings, you may have to assess the possible motivations of the initiator. Is this man perhaps having a sexual crisis and attempting to reaffirm his masculinity through you? If so, you might effectively deal with his advances with a gentle but direct response such as, "Dave you're an attractive fellow, but your very approach proves you're a total mismatch for me. Maybe you can find some woman who likes it."

Could it be that Dave actually has the hots for some other woman in your office and is trying to stir her jealousy with that age-old ruse? In which case a tack like this could head him off: "Thanks for the compliments, Dave. But why don't you give them to whomever they're really intended for?"

The most important principle in dealing with these kinds of attention situations is simply not to overreact, for to do so merely pours emotional fuel on them, doing no one any good. Again, the correct measure of detachment is indispensable.

Thus far we have considered mainly the qualitative aspects of attention. But can we stand to gain by thinking of it in *quantitative* terms, as implied in our metaphor of narcosis? The answer must be yes if attention is simply a depletable allotment of psychic energy. This idea is in fact close to the Eastern principle of the "reservoir of attention," a finite amount of psychospiritual energy available to the individual at any given moment. Psychologist Charles T. Tart's exhaustive research on consciousness lends empirical support to such a concept, and his hypothesis of "attention/energy" is usefully descriptive.

The twelfth-century philosopher-sage Al-Ghazzali pointed up the paramount importance of attention/energy as a resource that can be stored, refined, and increased in this life and made ready to be taken into the next. The afterlife aside, however, this great thinker emphasized that each of us is given only so much time on earth to attend to those things that are truly central to our life. The rest is chaff. Ghazzali's concerns about attention were essentially qualitative, however, dealing primarily with the development of perception and the stabilization of consciousness. He saw noncentral interests, preoccupations, and attachments as drawing off the reservoir of man's primal energy, which is transmutable into a refined, permanent form. Broadly, he is speaking of consciousness itself.

Al-Ghazzali's reflections on attention/energy are especially relevant today, for all of us in the modern world are to some extent victims of distraction. Demands on our attention rarely cease, all day long, at least in the cities. It is almost a cliché now that we so regularly suffer from sensory overload and brain benumbment. Only the recluse is exempt, but obviously isolation is an inadequate solution to the stress. Somehow we must find a way to conserve and utilize for more creative purposes the precious little mental energy we have to spend.

If we are too wrapped up in pursuing nonessentials, such as money and material possessions, we could be doing ourselves a great developmental disservice. Overindulgence in social activity, music, hobbies, television, sports, food, all sorts of diversions, and even our vocation can easily result in the imbalances and stresses that rob us of the energy we need for the quest of higher fulfillment. This is not to say that we should give up all such interests, for a correct amount of worldly endeavor is certainly requisite for that fulfillment. But a balanced perspective and sense of proportion is the means of determining what the amount should be.

So attitude is the key to regulating the input and output of attention in our lives, insuring that the impact of attention will be beneficial to us and those around us. Major psychospiritual traditions such as Zen Buddhism, Christian and Jewish mysticism, Vedanta, Sufism, and Taoism lay the groundwork for higher perception with the exercise of detachment. However, it is mental rather than physical detachment that is striven for. None of the authentics of these disciplines prescribe total-withdrawal from society or rejection of one's personal responsibilities therein. In fact, the opposite obtains: a deeper integration into human affairs through a fuller completion of oneself. At the same time, social conformity is transcended, and the superficialities of status and personality preening are effaced as a matter of course. That old attention/energy vampire, the ego, is reined in.

As we learn to consciously limit our attention to external objects and stimuli, we will find that we have much more energy left for internal uses. Beyond the immediately practical advantage of gaining extra layers of concentration, we will also find ourselves more able to monitor our thoughts and impulses. Self-observation is an art and science of its own, one that can be increasingly mastered over a lifetime. Following the ceaseless ebbs and flows of one's mind is not as easy as it may sound and certainly not accomplished by merely assuming the lotus position and droning "OM" with closed eyes, which is usually more a form of self-sleep than self-observation or genuine meditation. True self-observation in actuality requires consistently focused and regulated effort, in all kinds of situations, easy, difficult, or in-between. The first thing you learn is how surprisingly hard it is to sustain, even for a moment. Lest you become discouraged too soon, however, remember that you seldom know when you are learning or absorbing knowledge and often aren't when you think you are. That is an immutable principle of real learning, as distinguished from indoctrination, conditioning, and the like. Nonetheless, you will be able to notice small changes in yourself after a while, providing you do not seek them too strenuously. Uncritical acceptance of yourself *as is* is a precondition, and your improvements will subsequently manifest as gradual reductions in obsessive and compulsive tendencies, overemotionalism, rationalization, and negativism.

You may now have an inkling of the importance of attention as a factor in the equation of brain power. It is the light of your mental mill. If you decide to try channeling it into self-observation, it is wise to begin by watching its protean and subtle dynamics in the society around you. Take note of its give and take and the various conscious and unconscious ploys in which it is used to obtain objectives, personal and public. But remember also that, good or bad, attention is simply a fix. Too much of it can be lethal to the self as assuredly as overwatering or overlighting wilts a philodendron. However, what goes to pot in humans from overattention or misattention is not leaves and stems but the very roots of mental growth. The seduction of the limelight, as we all know, is that the limelight feels so good while we are in it, like basking in the sun on the beach. But we can get too much light, not being aware of our overexposure until the damage is done.

An interesting experiment you might want to perform to verify the narcotic nature of attention is simply to demand or withhold it in situations where you automatically give it or vice versa. For the giving can be as habitual as the receiving. You won't necessarily go into a cold sweat, but the discomfort will be there all the same. A caution: Don't try this where hostility or tension are already high or when the variables (people, mood, and so on) are so unknown as to constitute unneeded risk. Many bars, for instance, are not safe settings for more active forms of psychological research. Don't endanger your or anyone else's body or mind.

An accessible format for studying attention is to learn to merely notice it in the fleeting transactions of your daily life. Even outside the worlds of business and politics, attention is continually bartered and manipulated like a commodity. Don't we all know someone who monopolizes the conversation? One-to-one chitchat is commonly one-on-one competition, without our realizing it to be such, particularly when we ourselves are the competitors. Steering the topic his—or your—way is an artifice that most gabbers are totally unaware they have developed so highly. Even an exchange of one or two verbal passes can get the ball in our or their end of the court. "Scoring" can be achieved after a couple of fast opening fakes. A typical tactic is as follows:

Chit: I went to the State Fair yesterday.

Chat: Oh yeah . . . I went last week. The first week is the best week to go.

Chit: I saw Merle Haggard. He's better in person than on TV.

Chat: Uh-huh . . . I saw him last year. This time I saw Johnny Cash and the Carter family. I got my money's worth.

Chit: You did? They put on a good show, huh?

Chat: For sure, for sure. You missed a good one . . .

There you have it: attention mongering in its most casually effective form. It usually goes into further dimensions via feigned interest, perfunctory acknowledgment, and so on, but the upstaging is soon detectable in instances such as the above.

Do you allow attention/energy to "dope" your or someone else's ego, to foster your mental growth? Do you fritter it away on trivia and random distractions? If you do, the probable reason is that you are unknowingly avoiding the central issues of your life: your purpose for being, your real (not apparent) responsibilities to yourself and others, the necessities of love, psychological growth, and the reality of death. Only by learning how to focus your *full attention* when needed on these finally unavoidable matters will you begin to increase your mental powers of concentration, creativity, and inner, and outer harmony.

Note

1. Idries Shah, *Learning How to Learn: Psychology and Spirituality in the Sufi Way* (San Francisco: Harper & Row, Publishers, 1978).

Chapter Six

For Your Information

Strangely enough, it seems that the more information that is
made available to us, the less well informed we become. Decisions
become harder to make, and our world appears more confusing
than ever.... As more and more information is beamed at us,
less and less of it can be absorbed, retained and exploited. The
rest accumulates as dissipated energy or waste.

Jeremy Rifkin,
Entropy: A New World View

Life is a blur of Republicans and meat.
Zippy the Pinhead

If you are a baseball fan, possibly you enjoy the statistics—i.e.,
player and team standings—of the sport. But outside your game
world you may feel from time to time that you are being too
often "beaned" by the fast pitches of advertising, editorializing,
omnidirectional proselytizing, and political polemicizing from
right and left field. The mass media itself constitute a field full
of pitching machines throwing us fast balls, curves, and change-
ups. If you are a Republican, the blur of events and information
may seem to be coming disproportionately from Democratic
programs and rhetoric, such is the politicization of modern life.
If you are just anybody, there is probably too much verbal and

visual stimulation in general, to the point of subconscious distraction.

Idries Shah observes that "to drown in treacle [molasses] is as unpleasant as to drown in mud." Today people are drowning in information. He goes on to state, however, that drowning can be avoided if one knows how to *handle* information.[1] Perhaps you have never had the sensation of drowning at all. Still, it could well be, you are so used to the downpour and drizzle of words, images, and informational trivia that you aren't aware they are making mental mud, impedimental to progress in certain areas of your life. Most of us slosh through this daily bog of impressions and input less consciously than a native of the Everglades wades through swamp; we are totally conditioned to it. But unlike the literal one, the informational swamp is rising, with no end in sight. As we move from the industrial age into what social analysts now dub the communications or information age, many people are floundering in the quicksand of information, quite unsuspectingly in most instances. With the technological advances in information processing, we are all faced with an astronomical accumulation of data. Microfilm, microchips, computers, xerography, and other innovations contribute to an unprecedented onslaught on the human brain. Our mental muscle is stressed by overload, straining to sort it all out. "Technostress" may be hastening our whole society's collapse into the mire.

Information is wondrous stuff, necessary and very important stuff. We could not exist without the correct quantity and quality of it. In one sense the entire universe is a hologram of information, that is, an infinite network of communicative relations. Quantum physics, the genetic code (the DNA double helix and RNA), force fields such as electromagnetism, and gravity, animal communications, psychic phenomena (e.g., telepathy), and human emotions and speech are but a few examples of information systems. Knowledge itself is the highest form.

Yet there is an obverse negative to the positive process of information discharge: misinformation and overinformation. In a society accustomed to the "more is better" compulsion, the former problem is frequently acknowledged, the latter seldom. That they may go together hand in glove seems to be a curiously unrecognized possibility in the general population. Is that why the computer is so idolized? People who can spew out endless drivel of names and dates of people, places, things, and events are held in a high degree of awe. Enter the idiot savants. They are persons with very low IQs (usually due to genetic or developmental retardation) who, though typically unable to dress and feed themselves, tie their shoes, or carry on a meaningful conversation with someone, nevertheless can perform such marvels as tell you in a flash on what day of the week a monthly date (from 1 to 31) has occurred or will occur in any year. Some may be able to play an entire piano concerto after hearing it but once. All of them are capable of performing one singularly extraordinary mathematical or memory feat. Like many high-IQ experts in various fields, the idiot savant is *overspecialized*; he or she is the unlettered exaggeration of the absent-minded professor, the one-skill wizard. This recalls a current wisecrack—"He's got a photographic memory, but nothing ever develops."

If you take pride in being well informed, you might benefit by asking yourself if being thusly stuffed is hindering or helping you in developing real knowledge, particularly self-knowledge. If your cerebral circuitry is jammed with too much informational flotsam and jetsam, you may be giving up cognitive space that could be accommodating more useful input. While your brain's storage capacity can be gradually increased over time, through appropriate orientation of attention and perception, its powers of quantitative accommodation (of information) is finite at a given stage of development. So, when computerologists speak of "overflow" and "garbage in, garbage out," it might be instructive to extrapolate these meanings loosely to the brain itself.

One of the more definitive currents of modern times is the artificial intelligence boom. Since the Industrial Revolution we have increasingly occupied ourselves with inventing and designing machines to work for us—and imitate us. This trend has been highly advantageous from the labor-saving standpoint, with such devices as the telephone, television and radio, printing press, typewriter, tape recorder, phonograph, automobile, and airplane greatly facilitating speed and efficiency in communications (and transport in the last two inventions). The latest developments in the AI field have accelerated information processing and transfer beyond the wildest dreams of even the most visionary futurists of half a century ago. Now with the advent of computer/robots, which are rapidly displacing human workers in routinized occupations, "information" is taking on dimensions of influence somewhat foreign and almost incomprehensible to those unversed in AI. Many people who own or work with the new systems seem, even after the initial novelty has worn off, rather deferential to them. The "electronic brain" is likely to become more intimidating to underdeveloped humans as time goes on, through continuing refinement and sophistication. Mobile androbots (formerly known as drones) are at this very moment walking, talking, and doing almost as many things as large numbers of people do.

Yet it is at bottom absurd for any functional person to have an inferiority complex toward even the most dazzlingly efficient machine. Let alone paranoia—there are even fears of AI's taking us over. That could only happen with the collaboration and supervision of human masters, in which event it would not really be the machines that were gaining the uppermost hand. Relinquishing of personal autonomy and subordination of the self to the vested interests of mechanization have been speeded up by full-throttled technology, though the process shifted into gear with the Industrial Revolution.

To date no AI system has been devised to process information at any level even remotely approaching sheer human creativity. Think of all the great art masterpieces of such giants as Michelangelo, Rembrandt, Picasso, Monet, and Dali; the literature and poetry of Shakespeare, Euripedes, Homer, Wordsworth, Whitman, Hemingway, and Khayyám; the musical treasures of Beethoven, Mozart, Bach, Stravinsky, and Copland; the brilliant films of modern-day geniuses such as Fellini, Bergman, Woody Allen, and Steven Spielberg; the inventions of

Edison, Bell, the Wright brothers, Henry Ford; the scientific theories and discoveries of Pasteur, and the Curies, Salk, Einstein, and Darwin; the architectural triumphs of the world, from the Egyptian pyramids to the Parthenon and the Colosseum to Chartres Cathedral to the modern-day splendors of Sullivan and Wright. In the higher reaches of philosophy and psychology we have the likes of Plato, Marcus Aurelius, St. Augustine, Thomas Aquinas, Freud, Jung, Adler, Fromm, and Rogers, while the outstanding spiritual visionaries include the public figures of Jesus, Mohammed, Buddha, Moses, Lao Tze and many more who, as in the preceding categories, are omitted only because of lack of space or anonymity. Names could be dropped to encyclopedia length—the point of it all should be clear: The "information" involved in all of this genius and creativity extends into infinity. Are the rest of us so far behind this kind of brain power that we should relegate it to cerebral freakishness and allow our own intelligence to be butted out by RAM, ROM, and modem?

We ourselves are the true "mechanical marvels," if only we wouldn't take that fact for granted and take more vertical naps than we really need. From our development and understanding of cybernetics, however, we have learned reams of useful principles of mechanical information processing. The internal procedures by which the computer organizes and encodes information fed to it so that the data can be available on demand are crudely analogous to the human brain. The effect with which we are most concerned here is that popular (or unpopular) given described as "information overload." In *Entropy: A New World View* Jeremy Rifkin maintains that one result of this ceaseless verbal and visual flooding is the quickening of mental illness and breakdown. He notes that in just the last twenty years, mental health in the United States has grown into a $15 billion per annum industry, with one out of five (50 million) Americans now being treated for some form of emotional disorder. Rifkin underscores the parallel between "social pollution" and "emotional contamination."[2]

Somehow we have been led to believe that words, statistics, and wirephotos transmitted from officially sanctioned sources must always be nourishing information, something good for us in bulk. Such a misconception—a patently damaging one—is propagated by our educational system, which sees knowledge as something that can be served up and shoveled down cafeteria style. Data and theory are substituted for knowledge and understanding, packaged and overprocessed as a kind of informational offal. With the coming of the classroom computer, fact and data stuffing has been almost infinitely accelerated, with little or no concern whether the recipient can actually absorb and functionally store the many "bytes" that are poked down him. Nor is it considered what sense and use all of this information will make for in the nonacademic future of many students. To answer that the computer-filled future will require extensive versification in AI circularly begs the question.

In his valuable book *Use Both Sides of Your Brain*, Tony Buzan takes note of this information indigestion and observes that the only solution to the problem is "to learn new ways of handling and studying the information—new ways of using natural abilities to learn, think, recall, create, and solve problems."[3] This involves finding out more about how the human organism organizes and processes information in nonmechanized, innate modes. It could be that certain natural aptitudes have been schooled out of us and that we need to relearn *how to learn* what information is pertinent to our situation and how to apply it. In other words, what is needed is more real *knowledge*, not more random information.

The science of psychology has made useful contributions to our understanding of how the brain sorts out and stores for future reference the various environmental stimuli it has been conditioned to receive. That is quite a lot indeed in the hurly-burly of modern society. Interestingly enough, the problem of information overload plagues the behavioral sciences as much as other fields. With the number of psychologists increasing exponentially worldwide, there has been a concomitant—and may we say manic?—flooding of bookshelves and magazine racks with pop and academic psychological publications. There are literally thousands of different professional psychological journals available today, at least one hundred in the U.S. alone. With ever more professors publishing or perishing on the tightropes of their specializations, the competition among hairsplitting specialists and schools of thought far outstrips any practical value to the ordinary person. Abstruse hypotheses on linguistics and semantics (including analysis of nonsense syllables), schedules of reinforcement, stimulus exposures, shortterm versus long-term memory, spaced versus massed practice, in vivo desensitization versus systematic desensitization, and who knows what else, all amount to enough *furor scribendi* to drive any pragmatist off his or her head.

While the volume of psychological data is staggering, pragmatically applicable principles of memory, information processing, and learning can be counted on the fingers of one hand. This runaway inflation of psychological currency shows up in no end of printed facts and figures that are excessively trivial, essentially redundant, and even ludicrous. For example, beginning with a psychologist named Ebbinghaus in 1885, there have been roughly over five thousand studies on the memorization of nonsense syllables (these being experientially neutral words, usually consisting of three letters with a vowel in the middle, such as ZAL). But what have we found out beyond Ebbinghaus? Very little actually; mainly that people forget with time, that it is more difficult to learn lists of words if interfering factors are present, and that words at either the very beginning or end of such lists are remembered a bit more easily. These and a smattering of other ancillary findings are hard proof that restricted experiments are very much subject to the law of diminishing returns.

Nonetheless, there are many valuable studies in psychology, a good number yielding relevant information for the interested layperson. Perhaps what is now needed instead of more and more studies and publications is a pause for absorption and understanding of what it all means, a kind of input moratorium. We need to make more sense of that information which is already available to us. We need to find out how all of this data links up into a meaningful whole for us. What is crucial at present is the increasing of our comprehension, illumination, perception, insight, understanding, and knowledge.

What immediately practical measures can we take to begin screening out the dross of useless information from the input we really need? Well, having recognized the problem is a good start. Next, we simply need to *slow down* our intake. We all know that eating too fast is an unhealthy habit—why should reading, listening, or looking at visual messages be different? After reading everything in this chapter (and book), you may need to go back and retrace many of the ideas because of having sped over them too cursorily. There are many things we have to repeat to gain more grasp, more depth. If you pay no more than lip service to perception, understanding, and knowledge, then your efforts will be half-hearted and functionally empty. Ask yourself whether you really value quality over quantity and true insight over opinion based merely on data, or if you favor production without comprehension. If you are afflicted with the latter point of view, you certainly need to recognize your problem as a single case in the general contagion that has spread through the misinformed and misdiagnosed population.

Greed, overambition, and competition are causing many of us to choke on information in our haste to selfishly exploit every situation that comes our way. Getting back some breath of sanity may require doing whatever has to be done to improve our mental capacity to simply pay attention to our and others' real needs. This includes developing various skills and abilities: reading, listening, perception, attention, discrimination, thinking, memory, organization, control, motivation, concentration, visualization, imagination, articulation, and even creativity. Don't be bowled over by this extended list of positives; their cutting edge tends to be sharpened as a matter of course with the reduction of negative emotions. Phobias, prejudices, inflexibility, paranoia, depression, and the like, distort informational input and prevent its harmonious processing. This is where self-confidence and stress management are necessary, for without them the brain lacks the resiliency required for adjusting to and regulating environmental stimuli at large.

Finally, there is the possibility that heavy attendance to audio and visual electronics is literally a hard habit, perhaps a facet of a larger complex of an attention narcosis, as discussed earlier. As such, it could be a true "drug problem" on the same scale as with those substances that are taken orally and venously into the body. Whether eyes vacuously trained on the TV screen or glossed in vibrational ecstasy beneath a headset, the signs of cerebral benumbment and pupil dilation are often obvious. As far as we know, no extensive research has been done on the long-term effects of electronic stimulation on the human brain and physiology, although such studies would surely be worthwhile, perhaps surprising.

The next time you chance to turn on a radio or television, note the overpointed tones in which much advertising, editorializing, and generally effete verbosity is delivered to your ears. Even the most picayune news items are stressed as if they were major headlines. The air of urgency pervades most of broadcasting, jamming our brains and nervous systems with overloads of personal irrelevancies made to sound like something we should really know. Perspective and proportion are absent.

It is said that, on the average, one American in two does not read even one book a year. No wonder there are so many unpublished and part-time writers, so many excellent (and unexcellent) books being shipped back to warehouses after months of neglect on bookstore shelves. And for those people who do read there's always the current best-seller mania, but what of those informationally superb volumes that never get the attention that lesser publications often do because their authors are unknown or unpromoted?

As Idries Shah has pointed out, people often starve in the midst of plenty, not because they don't have enough information but because they do not know how to identify and use that which is at hand. For many of us a few good, correctly chosen books a year could be just what the head doctor might order. That and a little more electronic silence.

Notes

1. Idries Shah, *Reflections* (Baltimore: Penguin Books, 1972), p. 9.
2. Jeremy Rifkin, *Entropy: A New World View* (New York: Bantam Books, 1980).
3. Tony Buzan, *Use Both Sides of Your Brain.* New York: E. P. Dutton & Co., 1976), p. 111.

Chapter Seven

Open Mind

Here's a fact worth the knowing,
So treasure it and mark it well;
When the mind is through with growing,
Then the head begins to swell.

Anon.

When was the last time you were given "expert" advice, only to find out later that it wasn't even of good amateur quality? How often have you been given the wrong directions to a location by someone who sounded quite sure of himself? Our guess is, probably in recent memory.

We live in a society that seems to have an epidemic phobia of appearing ignorant. But there is no disgrace in being ignorant in itself. Staying ignorant of what is beneficial to know, when there is correct information available, is another matter. And here, perhaps, we have touched on the crux of the modern problem of the "swollen head"—*information.* After all, with all of this information in the air it is something of an ego shrinker, is it not? to not know something that others assume you know.

Yet we can't be privy to every public "fact" floating around—who would want to be? Nonetheless, many people feel inferior in the presence of those more "informed" or well-read than themselves. Never mind that the envied information may be useless for anything other than making social impressions; the fuel of much cocktail and coffee-house gib-gab. "Shooting the bull" is a legitimate outlet for everyone from time to time, but all too often the bull is a wasted carcass.

For those interested in rankings and ratings, the simple (and popular) one-to-ten model is offered below, in the interest of personal knowledgeability. Call it the Paracelsus scale. Paracelsus was a famous sixteenth-century German physician and philosopher who could not abide ignorance in the guise of erudition or pseudoknowledge of any stripe. He was an indefatigable seeker of truth, in medicine and outside it.

Rate yourself on the Paracelsus scale by circling a number.

10
9
8
7
6
5
4
3
2
1

Forget about your score for now. You may wish to change it later. There is a hidden score in this scale. If you detect it quickly, that may mean you are clever but not necessarily "knowledgeable."

Possibly the most formidable barrier to fuller use of the mind/brain is what is popularly and appropriately called closed-mindedness. Where blindness of the mind is caused by the corrosive effects of bias and prejudice on our perceptual windows, closed-mindedness is more akin to not acknowledging the need of cleaning those windows or perhaps not even opening them. Negativity, pessimism, deep prejudice, and arrogance are traits typical of this thrombosis of thought. Overattachment to the familiar and lack of imagination aid the process. The unfortunate condition is that of being a mental shut-in (often worse than physical confinement), with all the stifling air of rationalization and emotional frustration found in the occupants of dank and lightless habitations.

How can such a wondrous palace of possibilities as the human brain be reduced to a run-down prison of routinism? Who in their right mind would want to hang around looking at the Black Hole of Calcutta when they have yet to take in the splendors of the Taj Mahal? Ignorance may have a lot to do with it; you first have to know the Taj exists and then how to get to it if the possibility itself exists. But problems more common than ignorance are laziness and insecurity. We are a habit-oriented species, following the lines of least resistance. Darwinians would say that we evolved this proclivity because it maximized survival changes in primeval times when existence was a daily battle. Going a step too far into the bush could quickly invite an attack of teeth and claws. One fellow's being impulsively spontaneous or innovative might easily endanger the whole clan or tribe.

Dr. Edward deBono agrees with the survival explanation for the powerful "force of habit." He notes that the mind is habitually uncreative—it is usually preoccupied with organizing masses of incoming data into convenient patterns. Once the pattern is established, then the mind tends to rely upon that pattern in future situations, in order to facilitate decision-making and action in an otherwise complex world.[1] So the human brain is most adept at pattern making and constant use. That explains why, when the brain is presented with new ideas and information, its processing centers tend to screen out the really novel elements. The familiar parts are automatically selected out of the general concept, thus expediting the dismissal of the concept as old hat. Fear of the new is the reality, however.

Many people's thought patterns appear to be far more rigid than the mere pedestrian personality trait known as stubbornness. These individuals all share a bent toward highly structured lifestyles and ready deference to authority. According to psychologist Gordon Allport in *The Nature of Prejudice*, "The need for authority reflects a deep distrust of human beings." Authoritarian personalities may appear to be confident and self-assured, but this facade is easily breached by unexpected opposition, challenge, or even the presence of someone who dresses and behaves markedly differently. Suppressed hostility, low self-esteem, and high levels of anxiety and insecurity then emerge in signs of nervousness, avoidance, and outbursts of anger. Still, these weaknesses can be long camouflaged if the sources of friction are excluded from the environment.[2]

Another form of narrow-mindedness, which would seem to be quite unlike the authority type, is the panacea impulse— "Aha, we have it . . . this is it!" Social movements and schools of psychotherapy provide outstanding instances of this penchant for pat answers, leaping to conclusions and reluctance to let go of a good thing once it has outlived its (often short-lived) usefulness. People who are frustrated, unhappy, confused, or in pain frequently grasp in desperation at a Eureka! promise of a solution to their problem and hold on even after it has proven ineffective. If the attachment is to a "cause" of some sort, obsession is mistaken as single-mindedness and dedication and is exploited as such by their leaders.

Panacea thinking usually includes subscription to a particular belief system—a system that generically (1) oversimplifies and (2) tends to exclude alternative possibilities. Examples are legion, and no segment of the population, educated or not, is immune. Medical doctors, for instance, are preternaturally determined to find a physical cause for every disorder. In psychiatry the etiology for such illnesses as schizophrenia and dementia is based almost solely on organic and biochemical models. Over the past three decades numerous biochemicals have been tagged as the probable causes of schizophrenia, eventually to be disproven. Alzheimer's disease is considered to be largely genetic, when in fact there could be environmental and nutritional factors present that at least exacerbate the syndrome (elderly people are often *expected* to become senile, aren't they?). And of course, the treatments for many of these pathologies are heavily physical ones: medication, electroshock, surgery.

In the unhappy halls of education, a significant number of educators and parents are convinced that most of our children's academic problems are due to too much emphasis on arts and humanities studies. "Back to basics" (the three Rs) is their rallying cry, with no-nonsense discipline also touted as the cure-all for what ails these miseducated kids. Simplisms that are summed up in short slogans are perhaps those we should be most wary of. In high levels of government we see the same kind of squint-minded outlooks on complex phenomena. Example: From the time he was elected, to the middle of 1984, American president Ronald Reagan and his administration expended 85 percent of their time trying to remedy the economy. In focusing so much concern and energy on money, goods, and their distribution, the implication is that, should the economy improve, America will be displaying its greatness, and our major problem will be diminished. The panacea is the material one of supply-and-demand prescription. But the government is not alone in thinking that decreased unemployment, greater profits, and consumer clout mean happiness for all; most polls taken between 1980 and 1984 listed the economy as the people's main concern. Other key issues such as the threat of nuclear war and environmental degradation followed far behind.

The contemporary "human potentials movement" has packed more promised cures than a traveling medicine show, with as many labels: TM (Transcendental Meditation), promoted as a psychotherapeutic tool, the answer to stress, and a release to spiritual freedom, turned out to be simply a trick of autosuggestion; health foods, vegetarianism, macrobiotics, jogging, and aerobics have been fervently pushed as vehicles to physical and mental health. There are the highly specialized techniques of rolfing, acupressure, acupuncture, Feldenkreis, psychocybernetics, bioenergetics, hypnosis, and postural integration. The outer fringes include astrology, the I Ching, dervish dancing, UFOlogy cults, tarot cards, and among numerous other extra-Gileadan balms, the "Course in Miracles."

In the more sophisticated markets of establishment psychology and psychiatry (where the Ph.D. and M.D. shingles are hung out), we have the multitudinous schools of personality theory and psychotherapy. Albert Ellis's rational therapy offers to reason your mental and emotional ills right out of you, Janov's primal therapy to scream them out, Berne's transactional analysis (TA) to role play them out. Rogers's self-therapy, Glasser's reality therapy, Leonard Orr's rebirthing (emotionally, of course), assertiveness training, behavior therapy, Erhard's *est*, scientology, and many such packages stock the shelves of pop psychology. With tongue astutely in cheek, R. D. Rosen (*Psychobabble*) observes, "The problem is not that so many people are constantly looking for enlightenment these days, but that so many are constantly finding it."[3]

The quality of all this "enlightenment" is not rigorously examined in the light of any objective standard—perhaps it cannot be. But the "quality control" in many of these practices is virtually nonexistent, and most of the practices are especially subject to exploitation by charlatans and misuse by well-meaning inepts. This is even more the case with imported esotericism: the guru-cult phenomenon. "Marketing the mystic East" or "karma cola," as author Gita Mehta tags it, is a lucrative business made possible by the spiritual voids left by the bankruptcy of much of religious orthodoxy and materialistic science. Many of the disenchanted have turned to drugs and, while getting a glimpse of another reality, realize the high doesn't last and must be attained some other way. Having heard that there are nonchemical paths to enlightenment, which originated in the East, a number of the desperate, monied seekers make long treks to Oriental locales, enrolling in monasteries or ashrams. Some return disillusioned. Most, however, can find a guru and a discipline right here in the West. There's Yogi Bhajan and 3HO, Maharishi and TM, Majaraj-Ji and Divine Light Mission, Hare Krishna, Da Free John and his Laughing Man Institute, Bhagwan Shree Rajneesh, Reverend Moon and his Unification Church, and a bazaarful of others, often associated with traditional practices or established religious such as Yoga (hatha, tantra, karma, bhakti, raja, japa, kundalini), Hinduism, Zen Buddhism, Baha'i, Vedanta, and Taoism.

The severe and obvious problem of the kinds of "systems" listed above is that they are effectively cults, of no actual developmental value. The container (exotic exercises and dress) is empty of most nutritional content. The gurus who preside over them, however, assure their "disciples" that they are on their way to spiritual enlightenment (or are standing at the threshold), whereas in reality what is taking place is attention therapy. The gurus are the therapists, though are themselves often self-deceived, wholly believing in their imagined spiritual ascendancy. They may be money or power hungry, unconsciously or not. In a few cases they are outright frauds. Usually gurus are quite intelligent, with high skills of manipulation. Their talents are for the most part misused; instead of nurturing the illusions of their followers, they could be helping them with truthful guidance counseling, group therapy, and the like.

Almost all enrollees in cults lack the information that would aid them in diagnosing themselves or their guru as deluded. Certainly the gurus have no teaching qualifications as advertised. Few cultists understand the essence of a true spiritual teaching situation; total adaptation to the local culture and the goal of increasing the student's general capacities for a more creative integration into that culture. Many years of preparation, of learning how to learn, are required for this task, entailing living and working in society as usual. Stock externals such as Oriental clothing and special diets are avoided as nonfunctional anachronisms, along with such diversions as routine fasting, dancing, breathing, and meditative exertions, and posturing of all kinds. This is not to say that such activities are never pursued in any valid context; they are, but in that context have little or no resemblance to the popular trappings of cults. And the real practices do not conform to stereotypical notions of "spirituality" and sanctity.

It should be fairly obvious now, from just the few examples cited above, that closed-mindedness can take liberal as well as conservative forms. Whether the shut mental windows are on the West or the East, whether it is the miserliness of Ebenezer Scrooge or the ropes of credulity of Lemuel Gulliver, constraint of thought and behavior is the uncreative result. The panacean paradigm seems to have become pervasively institutionalized in modern times, with some help from high technology. It's a little like the seduction of oversimplified computer software; you can get so involved with the limiting operations of a program that you forget about new programs altogether. Part thinks it's whole.

"Opportunity only knocks once" may be one of the most misleading half-truths ever turned off the tongue of an epigramist. Much more likely, opportunity is continually knocking on many closed doors and windows. Once in a while we hear the knock but are too lazy or distracted to answer. Or we answer too late, perhaps at the wrong portal. In his book *Opportunities*, Dr. deBono elaborates on a phenomenon-concept he calls "opportunity search." While oriented to the business world, the various principles he discusses are widely applicable to any kind of enterprise demanding the recognition and development of new ideas—ideally to life in general. The reason, says deBono, that many opportunities pass us by is a *perceptual* one: We do not recognize an opportunity for what it is.[4]

Life is full of opportunities. Unfortunately, we frequently get so entangled in cross-purposes and confusion that we do not see opportunities even when they are at our feet. And this is not true only of the so-called underachievers in life. Many success stories have their share of "the ones that got away." For instance, Alexander Graham Bell once offered Western Union all of his telephone patents for the comparatively small sum of $100,000 and was turned down. Today AT&T is one of the largest and richest corporations in the world. When it was first perfected, the Xerox process was offered for sale to IBM and Kodak, only to be rejected by both. But Xerox chairman John Davies, then an executive of an obscure British company known as the Rank Organization, realized its potential, and the rest is duplication history. Ditto the birth-control pill: developer Russell Marker could not find a pharmaceutical firm to buy his product, so with the help of fiscal backers went on to form the highly successful Syntex Corporation.

People in all types of creative fields like to think of themselves as always discriminative and open-minded, but enough Scrooges and Gullivers appear in the history of art, entertainment, invention, science, and medicine to prompt serious doubts. The movie script for *Jaws* was rejected by 20th Century Fox as financially unpromising but later picked up by Universal where it was turned into a record money-making film. The very next year the *Star Wars* screenplay was turned down by Universal and taken by Fox. In 1962 Decca Recording Company showed the Beatles the door, stating: "We don't like their sound. Groups of guitars are on the way out." When Fred Astaire first tripped the light fantastic to Hollywood, he was put down as only "a balding, skinny actor who can dance a little." Bette Davis, Clark Gable, and Brigitte Bardot all failed their early screen tests.

If the contemporary critics of such musical and literary giants as Brahms, Gertrude Stein, and Emily Dickinson had had power of absolute censorship, thousands of unique masterpieces might have been lost to the world—never mind household names. The following quotes speak inelegantly for themselves: "I played over the music of that scoundrel Brahms. What a giftless bastard!" (and this from Peter Ilich Tchaikovsky, himself a renowned composer). "She [Emily Dickinson] is a half-cracked poetess." (editor Thomas Wentworth Higginson, the *Atlantic Monthly*, 1837). Today Dickinson's poems rank with the classics. Likewise, the verse of E. E. Cummings was rejected by over a dozen publishers, until it was finally published by—his mother. Ernest Hemingway's first short stories were also rejected. Creative bias has not abated to this day. Dr. Wayne Dyer's book *Your Erroneous Zones* was self-published after nearly two dozen publishers dismissed it as too great a marketing risk. To date it has earned over $5 million.

You would think that a low rate of closed-mindedness is inherent and pragmatically necessary in science and technology. Necessary, yes—inherent, no, if we look at the uphill battle so many inventors have had to wage against establishment captiousness. These several cases are but too true stereotypes among recorded hundreds: "The speculation . . . is interesting, but the impossibility of ever doing it is so certain that it is not practically useful." (Editor of *Popular Astronomy* to rocket pioneer Robert Goddard's proposal of considering nuclear power, 1902). "Flight by machines heavier than air is unpractical and insignificant, if not utterly impossible." (astronomer Simon Newcomb, eighteen months before the Wright brothers flew). After hearing about the Wrights' airborn success, Newcomb alluded to "unfair trickery" and pronounced that, even if it were true, it would still be impossible for an aircraft to carry a passenger along with the pilot. "Very interesting, Whittle, but it will never work!" (professor of aeronautical engineering at Cambridge University to Frank Whittle, developer of the jet engine in the early twenties).

Have you ever flipped through the *Book of Lists*? Many of the entries therein are testaments to mind lag. Take the following instances of lengthy time lapse between invention (or conception) and popular use (from vol 1): antibiotics (1910/1940), frozen foods (1908/1923), heart pacemaker (1928/1960), helicopter (1904/1941), nuclear energy (1919/1965), photography (1782/1838), radar (1904/1939), radio (1890/1914), silicone (1904/1942), television (1884/1947), zipper (1883/1913).[5] Why, for example, television took so long to gain acceptance is reflected in the negative assessment of a *New York Times* writer who held forth that "the problem with television is that people must sit and keep their eyes glued to the screen: the average American family hasn't time for it. Therefore the showmen are convinced that for this reason, if no other, television will never be a serious competitor of broadcasting."[5] If only he had been right . . . now, forty-five years and millions of screen-glued eyes later, it is not hard to see why critics have often been called cranks, particularly in the arts and sciences. Some critics are perfect "reverse barometers." Yet criticism can be invaluably constructive—without skeptical capacity every last one of us would be a Gulliver.

So it looks as if an opportunity is not always as plain as the nose on one's face, even when it is drawn up and patented. "An opportunity," says Dr. deBono, "exists only when you can see it." His concept of "opportunity search" may not sound that new on the face of it, but he has actually devised innovative and effective strategies that allow one to become more opportunity conscious, and hence more open-minded, far beyond the passive rationality generally meant by that phrase.

The majority of people are not opportunity conscious, and there are several interrelated reasons. One reason is that the methods of our educational system have not fundamentally changed since the Middle Ages. The emphasis has always been on training in *established* knowledge—reading, writing, arithmetic, geography, anatomy, history. Logic and memory are highly valued functions. But none of this draws on creativity, imagination, innovation; opportunity consciousness requires just these capacities, along with the ability to think laterally. The latter is a nonlogical (not "illogical") mode of exploring possibilities and developing ideas. Scores of great discoveries and inventions (including some of those listed above) thought to be totally fortuitous are, in fact, the product of lateral thinking. Although random factors do operate here, the general process can be consciously exploited. The serendipity element can be amplified.

The key to lateral thinking is the flexibility required for changing one's mental direction or focus, in an instant if need be. DeBono provides a comely example: A man has an eye for blonds and happens to spot one across a crowded party room. Straightaway he begins strategizing a way to get an introduction to her. His brain so buzzes with this scheming that he does not even notice another tall, even more attractive blond just over his shoulder. His fixated focus would not take notice of this second blond should she be breathing in his ear. This simple inability to switch direction of attention is a severe detriment in many areas of life and is called obsession when the other person has it.

Once again we can see how rigid mental and behavioral patterns—i.e., beliefs, attitudes (especially negative), habits, mental sets, and assumptions—prevent the perception of possibilities. In the context of the above case, they even preclude the new input in which such perceptions take place. Not only that, they dictate the kinds of questions we ask, even when we admit to a problem. Consider, for instance, the possible difference between "What *more* can I do?" and "What *else* can I do?" There may be something more than semantic nitpicking in the distinction. And then of course there are those people who seldom or never ask questions, so snug and smug are they with their status quo. No rocking the boat for them—until they reach that cataract dead ahead.

Everyone of us can become more open-minded. But what is the method? You may already understand that there are no step-by-step recipes. Also, the process is a lifelong cultivation; it is not "Voilà—"I'm open-minded!" A possible start is to take an inventory of your most taken-for-granted assumptions and oldest ideas—about yourself, others, life, and the universe. Take your time—days, weeks, or months if need be. Next, you might read about real-life cases of closed-mindedness in such sources as biographies and histories. Try finding them as well in the daily news and events in your community. The examples above are taken from (besides the *Book of Lists #1*) *Rejection* by John White and *Facts and Fallacies* by Chris Morgan and David Langford.[6]

Reading outside your usual sphere(s) of interest is an excellent and easily accessible way of getting a wedge into closed-off areas of your mind. Very often what seem to be unrelated phenomena have underlying and interesting connections. One area of knowledge can give you a broader slant on another. For instance, if you are a decorator you might get some inspirational ideas from just leafing through an illustrated text on botany or zoology, with their fabulous natural designs. And, who knows? You could become interested in plants or animals for themselves. If you are well read in the social or political sciences, science fiction may offer you some perspectives that your regular fare does not. And do you spend as much time reading alternative points of view as you do your own?

Thus far we have discussed only diurnal closed-mindedness. But what about the one-third of your life you spend in the protean world of sleep? Do you assume that your mind closes when your eyelids do, that your inner life must slip into suspended animation soon after the shades are pulled down?

Or that those baffling extravaganzas called dreams are nothing more than the far-out fringes of your daytime fantasies, hopes, and fears? Or that insomnia is always a "sleep disorder"?

We have a lot to learn about sleep and dreams—even the experts do. Research in this fascinating field has accelerated over the past few decades. You are probably aware that dream interpretation is something of a going concern (pioneered in Western psychology by Sigmund Freud), and perhaps that it purports to provide the means to unraveling the psychic imbroglios of neuroses, repressed sexual impulses, sublimations, and shadowy meanings of all sorts. Dreams have naturally been a stock in trade of the occultists, who are common to most cultures. Today research into paranormal phenomena (telepathy, remote viewing, psychokinesis, and so on) is verifying the ancient belief that the state we call sleep is one in which incredible—sometimes awesome—energies of the psyche are automatically released, for good, ill, or any combination thereof. For the present purpose we need only consider the potential of this subterranean power source to be harnessed for brain/mind expansion.

On bookstore shelves today you can find a wide array of books dealing with psychic phenomena, some specializing in how to exploit your dream life. These books run a spectrum of quality from nearly useless to modestly helpful. In our view, however, no such handbooks should solely be used as trustful guides to your "hidden life." For instance, you may find a number of author/dream merchants instructing you to keep a running inventory of your dreams, faithfully recording all you can remember upon awakening. Advice on detecting motifs, concealed themes, and symbolism will likely be included. However, be also advised that these exercises demand more than a little time and can easily run into complications. Like a common intuition, a dream is often an amorphous, elusive thing, which can be lost if pursued too hard.

Yet we all have impressive dreams from time to time and too little recall power to run them again when our eyes and mind open back on daylight reality. If you feel that you have had a dream of significance, perhaps a recurring one, you may stand to gain by remembering as much of it as possible and writing it down. The dream's general texture and tone may give you clues to important things that need to be focused on and/or corrected. The subconscious is a vast and deep dimension of human existence, but we cannot live there in waking life. Therefore, to take dreams too seriously or allow them to become sources of anxiety will disorder that life. We can apply a good deal of common sense to these experiences, like any other. It is probably best not to search too hard for direct connections between dreams and actual occurrences, though that is not to say that such connections do not exist.

Sleep and dreams have always provided artists, inventors, and creative workers of all stripes with cornucopias of ideas and visions for their work. Thumb through the autobiographies of some of these cerebral dynamos and you will find credit for great discoveries, theories, and masterpieces given to revelations received during slumber or just before or after it (hypnogogic states). Quirks of insights during daydreams and fantasies have been seized and amplified into knowledge. Entire symphonies, paintings and novels have been composed with closed eyes (later to be materially produced) and, no less, inventions and scientific and medical breakthroughs. Edison disclosed that many of his ideas came immediately on awakening from his regular catnaps. The mathematician Poincare actually visualized what turned out to be an important set of numerical combinations while just on the verge of sleep, after he had been drinking coffee. Einstein was an inveterate daydreamer (was reprimanded for it in school) and stated that "the really important thing [in science] is intuition."

The enigmatic logic of the subconscious mind and the testimony of so many geniuses, then, show that insomnia may not be the Great Curse of Sleep in every instance. It may simply signal that there are mental energies stirring that refuse to sleep while there is still work to be done, decisions to be made, or problems to be solved. Or ideas to be had. Insomnia can be a very opportune time to make connections.

At this juncture you may wish to score yourself on the Paracelsus scale again. Possibly you noticed something peculiar about the scale, something missing? Yes, there is no frame of reference, no relative values given for the numbers. So, if you scored yourself, say, a 7, does that mean you are seven times more knowledgeable than a 1, or seven times more ignorant? And *whom* are you measuring your knowledge against—the gang at the office, the boys at the club, your debating team, Plato, or Pogo? Remember, too, that we invited only *those inter- ested* to rate themselves. The "hidden score" stays hidden.

You're right: The Paracelsus scale is a red herring. But there are shoals of red herrings swimming about in our brains daily. They're called assumptions.

> He who knows not, and knows not that he knows not, is a fool— shun him.
>
> He who knows not, and knows that he knows not, is a child— teach him.
>
> He who knows, and knows not that he knows, is asleep—wake him.
>
> But he who knows, and knows that he knows, is a wise man— follow him.
>
> Proverb

> Knowledge is in stating ignorance.
> Proverb

Notes

1. Edward deBono, *The Use of Lateral Thinking* (London: Jonathan Cape, 1967), p. 16.
2. Gordon Allport, *The Nature of Prejudice* (Garden City, N.Y.: Anchor/ Doubleday, 1958).
3. R. D. Rosen, *Psychobabble* (New York: Avon Books, 1979), p. 245.
4. Edward deBono, *Opportunities* (Baltimore: Penguin Books, 1980).
5. David Wallechinsky, Irving Wallace, and Amy Wallace. *The Book of Lists.* New York: Morrow, 1977.
6. John White, *Rejection* (New York: Addison Wesley Publishing Co., 1982); Chris Morgan, and David Langford, *Facts and Fallacies* (New York: St. Martin's Press, 1981).

Chapter Eight

Freedom

No man is free who is not master of himself.

Epictetus

Men are free when they are in a living homeland . . . not when they are escaping to some wild west. The most unfree souls go west and shout of freedom. Men are freest when they are the most unconscious of freedom. The shout is the rattling of chains . . . always was.

D. H. Lawrence

Throughout history humans have been obsessed with the pursuit of freedom. Declarations of independence, manifestos, bills of rights, and national constitutions have trumpeted this ideal and engraved it in stone. We equate freedom, correctly so, with our inalienable right not to be unjustifiably confined, shackled, censored, or hampered in any way. Progress toward its external realization has been irresistible, though haplessly slow. We are apt to forget that it was only a century and a quarter ago that the Negro slaves were freed in the United States, a country always looked upon as the freest in the world. Around the world today there are large numbers of people, even outside prisons and jails, whose speech and actions are severely curtailed. The evening news sometimes gives us a fleeting reminder of their existence.

But beyond physical freedom lies mental freedom. Have you ever considered that having the former without the latter is more meaningless than vice versa? History itself indicates that physical fetters are after the fact of mental ones. And so with current events. Few of us stop to think that we may be slaves to our own psyche. All the while we are plumping for freedom we could be unaware that we are obsessing ourselves or others with the very idea of it, thereby locking our energies into its image so that we have too little left to achieve its reality.

There are numerous poignant parallels between the "security" of modern life and prison. The shared factor is *routine*; in prison the bars are made of steel; in life on the ouside they are the invisible restraints of habit, social rounds, and keeping up appearances. We outsiders unconsciously chafe against our disguised confinement as fitfully and futilely as prisoners behind bars do. The main difference is that "doing time" is generally a more conscious state of mind when you are literally locked up.

The achieving and feeling of freedom both seem to be bound up with the sense of dimension. *Inner space* hints at this elusive perceptual function, but as another of those fuzzy buzz terms, it connotes little more than yogish airheadedness. An incisive and entertaining treatment of the dimensional sense is Edwin Abbott's perennially instructive tale *Flatland*, written over a century ago.[1] Dubbed "a romance of many dimensions," it concerns a civilization of curious two-dimensional creatures living in a multidimensional world (our universe). These "Flatlanders" perceive reality only in their two dimensions, although it is a metaphor and we assume that their two-dimensional (width and length) bodies are descriptive of all terrestrial illusion. But their logic is uncomfortably similar to our own and too, too real indeed. For life takes on curious limitations when it is lived perpetually before-the-nose. Since the dimension of height is unknown to the Flatlanders, it is likewise unthinkable to them that a visitor could come from another world; for them another world could not exist because they cannot conceive of "up." As geometrical beings, they determine their individual social status by their number of angles. A simple line is the lowest caste; polygons the highest, which is the hierarchy of priests. The goal of ultimate perfection is to become a circle, godlike. But error is incipient in this scheme: Since only one side of a person-figure can be approached at a time, women are taken to be lines when they are in fact circles. "What is your angle?" is the question every male asks of every other. Discernment of angular status by degree of brightness is by itself unreliable, and "feeling" one's way around others is literally the social modus operandi.

The Flatland story takes an interesting twist when a three-dimensioner descends from Spaceland and with difficulty makes contact with a cerebrally receptive Flatlander. A labored kind of Socratic dialogue ensues, with the host at last acknowledging the reality of his spherical guest, bidding him farewell in awe and mystery. However, after reporting this visitation to his bright, sympathetic nephew, he is found out by the authorities and committed to an asylum to live out his last days. Much more than an airy parable, this brief masterpiece is a sketch of our own perceptual prison. Is it possible that we are essentially Flatlanders who are fortunate enough to have an extra dimension to know about?

"Two men looked out from prison bars," runs a verse, "One saw mud, the other stars." Assuming we find a window in our prison to look out of, how useful can it be to allow ourselves to become hypnotized by stars or mud? After all, there is an entire world between, one that may be far more relevant to our escape if we are needlessly incarcerated. On the other hand, surveying the stars or mud might yield some benefit to that purpose beyond the optimism or pessimism meant in the poem. Habitual expectations, assumptions, thoughts, ideas, and actions are the "coercive agencies," as Idries Shah calls them, that bar us from real freedom, even though we proclaim liberty in the streets and get it in writing.

So we begin to see that the key to freedom lies in consciousness itself. One can turn the key(s) by asking important questions, not always as easy as you may think under most conditions. "What does this mean?" and "Where does this get us?" are the kinds of question we seldom dare ask out loud around others and have consequently grown afraid of asking ourselves. Which is proof that we moderns have to live with taboos as surely as primitives do. And of course we have our totems too, albeit they are not on poles. One such is "common sense," which as Shah has noted, is frequently neither. Take a time-wrinkled example: *creativity*. Studies of children prove conclusively that all of us are born with creative potential, but that enculturation, including a wide array of unfounded beliefs (common-sense myths), fixes our self-image so early and completely that by age twenty-five our social personality and status are finished for life. Whether we like it or not, we have slipped into a precast cultural mold and remain trapped in it because, like most others yoked in mediocrity, we have never learned to question such crucial truisms as "Some people are just born that way," "It's all in the genes," "You can't change fate," and "You'll never make it" (usually worded differently). Aligned with these kind of you-can'tisms are other fallacies such as "Play is for kids, work for adults" and the freezing fear of being wrong. Because the key of questioning is not discovered and used, the mind locks stay on; innovation, invention, and creative expression are stultified; and who knows what unimaginable amounts of intelligence and genius are wasted in brain cells inside and outside of jail cells?

Gail and Snell Putney in their insightful book *The Adjusted American* assert from their findings that most Americans do not understand their personal needs, do not as a rule fulfill them, and are therefore surfeited with anxiety and tension.[2] Thus being "well adjusted" means being neurotic in a society whose values and attitudes have become increasingly denaturalized. Materialism and consumerism have taken an unhealthy hold on the American mind, resulting in ubiquitous patterns of overcompetitiveness, greed, jealousy, envy, selfishness. Missing or in short supply are humanistic and spiritual qualities—altruistic cooperation, sympathy, magnaminity—resulting in a blockage of truer self-needs, intricately connected with those of others. The failure of inner self-actualization is mirrored in, perhaps in large part caused by, the importance attached to appearance. It is so paramount to *look* good that *feeling* good about oneself has also taken on narcissistic connotation, as evidenced in much of the physical-fitness movement. Waxing witty, well informed, and "self-aware" have hit such lows of superficiality that perception, sensitivity, intuition, and empathy have become meaningless notions in their wake.

Imbalances of the personality are the trammels of personal freedom. No need to reel off a list of History's Greatest Villains—it is the hordes of invisible little tyrannies, masses of mental barnacles that weigh us down and prevent us from scaling the prison walls to freedom. "Security" is a fine thing, providing it is the security of inner harmony and correct perspective rather than the confines of self-aggrandizement, materialistic and mental attachments, possessiveness . . . well, just leave it as the Seven Security Sins.

So it is indispensably helpful for each of us to rethink the ideal and the reality of freedom, to try to feel beyond the concept to the actuality, in the situations that daily test the limits of our mental and physical mobility. How many times a day do you look at your watch without realizing you are doing so? The time trap is perhaps the most unconscious and insidious of all in our overclocked and calendared culture. Instead of pouring our lives into the present moment, we merely exist for the next hour, day, week, or even year. So doing, we lose the present as well as the past and future by letting our purpose and energy leak away in time diffusion. We treat time like another consumer commodity, mistakenly assuming we can always buy more when it runs out.

An express purpose of such esoteric practices as meditation and yoga is to transcend the experience of space and time in one's consciousness. But for some people that may be equivalent to putting the cart ahead of the horse; for higher, truer experiences in these dimensions are necessary for developing advanced perception, intuition, and the like. Attempting a quantum leap from clock time to space-timeless nirvana may be detrimental to this process, resulting in but vapid metaphysical sensations. For the most part, Eastern mystical systems should be approached with caution. The aspirant can avoid possible self-deception by asking and reasking what his or her true motive is in this interest, as well as that of whoever is offering the mystical goods. If you yourself are such a seeker, consider that what you are seeking may simply be periodic respite from your daily grind. For that, a hobby such as astronomy, hiking, or skin diving might just fill the bill for you, not only expanding your sense of dimension but teaching you something about yourself as a vital part of the natural world.

True freedom entails freedom from obsessions, compulsions, and habit. While we could list several pointers that might serve you in your quest for mental freedom, a great amount of guidance and brain food is contained in the following, provided by Idries Shah.

COERCIVE AGENCIES

Make it your business to study in your life and in your surroundings:

The growth, development and activity of informal coercive agencies, not often recognised as such because of the poorly delineated identification and measurement tools in current use.

Such tyrannies, seldom have guns, clubs, centralised propaganda machines, uniforms and recognisable officials.

If you set up an experiment in any expectation, this expectation becomes a coercive agency whose attempts to lead you to certain conclusions you will have to take into account. Certain customs, social pressures, personal predilections, even individual decisions, can become coercive agencies in your life.

One of the reasons why man struggles against what he takes to be undesirable is that he unconsciously recognises the coercive influences in the surroundings and in himself. He then chooses a measurable form of them, to satisfy and therefore "abolish" his need to resist or frustrate them.

He has in so doing, of course, only begged the question.

Thoughts, circumstances, the social milieu, a hundred and one things, can provide as powerful coercive agencies as anything that the human being can point to as a "despotism," or "tyranny."

A set of misunderstood ideas or practises may become such a tyranny. A group of people who deal with each other with the greatest kindness yet who perform practises or carry out other activities unsuitable for their development are such an agency.

The tyranny of ideas or practises is far subtler and more effective than the avowed repressive institution because the participants are not aware that they are being constrained. The extreme case, the man who spends all his time shouting "I'm free, I tell you!" is not free, because of lack of time, to do anything other than shout "I'm free!"

Certain coercive agencies have become indispensable to the victims. People with closed minds or small ranges of thought and action depend for their pleasures upon the rewards offered by obedience to the coercive agency. If this obedience is couched in the form of "disobedience," they feel that they are not coerced.

Such people cannot make progress towards their mental liberation at one bound. Their world has to be made larger, and to be seen to be larger, before they can take any step beyond their narrow life.

There is no repression like that of the man who causes his own, in the name of freeing himself. Since he cannot attribute it to any outside source, and since he cannot see himself suppressing himself, he may very well be lost. He is already under the duress of "Slavery is freedom." It is interestingly indicative of his state that he fears loss of freedom while he has already lost it. He does this because—like a child—if he has lost something and merely pretends that he might lose it, this implies that he has still got it.

We need not talk of social action, politics nor economics, nor even sociology in this matter. The individual, and groupings of people, have to learn that they cannot reform society in reality, nor deal with others as reasonable people, unless the individual has learned to locate and allow for the various patterns of coercive institutions, formal and also informal, which rule him. No matter what his reason says, he will always relapse into obedience to the coercive agency while its pattern is within him.

This is one reason why you see people converted from one system of belief or practise to another: they are aware of the shortcomings of the first; they can pretend that the second, because it does not have the outer defects to which he takes exception, is "true," when the former was "not true."

The Study of Coercive Agencies and Man is what I would call this effort.[3]

Notes

1. Edwin A. Abbot, *Flatland* (New York: Dover Publications, 1952).
2. Gail and Snell Putney, *The Adjusted American* (New York: Harper & Row, Publishers, 1966).
3. Idries Shah, *Caravan of Dreams* (London: Octagon Press, 1968), pp. 197–99.

Chapter Nine

Whole Mind

Most of us have by now heard the term *holistic.* As psychologist Robert Ornstein has observed, it is one of those overinflated pop-isms that have prematurely outlived their usefulness because so much hot air has been pumped into them by "New Age" zealots and profiteers. Still, the idea behind the term represents a reality of primal importance to the brain and even to life itself.

The hyperrationalistic basis for modern science and Western education was in large part laid down by the French philosopher René Descartes in the seventeenth century. Descartes propounded what he saw as an essential dichotomy between mind and body, summed up in his famous "I think, therefore I am." He did much to clarify the philosophy of scientific method and helped usher in the modern scientific revolution.

As valuable as the Cartesian paradigm has been in the development of technology in our civilization, it has mechanized all thinking on the phonomenon of consciousness itself, splitting mind and body in an artificial dualism. Consequently, oversimplistic concepts and assumptions about both have resulted in a diminished idea of Man and Woman. Up to the present day intelligence has been relegated exclusively to the brain, the seat of analytic modes of reasoning. Examine almost any contemporary text on the topic of intelligence, and you will find the usual definition of IQ, that it is to be determined upon the ability for abstract reasoning, analytic aptitude, and scholastic readiness.

While these classroom skills have their valid uses, recent research on the split brain suggests that there is much more to creative cognition than was previously thought. The various findings conclusively point to the left hemisphere of the brain as the locus of reasoning in the abstract, verbal/symbolic manipulation, and analysis. In contradistinction, the right hemisphere is primarily involved with perception, imagination, synthesis, and intuition. The concept of intelligence is being expanded to include also all forms of creative capacity, social skill (tact, interpersonal perception), "street smarts," common sense, visual thinking power, and openness to new learning experiences. Prejudice, bias, obsession, culture-based fixations, and absence of motivation, self-confidence, self-image, relaxation, and concentration are being discovered as key variables in thinking (or not thinking) clearly and putting one's brain to better work.

Equating intelligence with what can be scored on a piece of paper is a much too narrow perspective on the brain/mind's potential. Fortunately, this is being recognized by more and more educators and psychologists, albeit there is a long way to go. We should bear in mind as well that there is much more to the human brain than just the left and right cerebral cortex, the topmost and most recently evolved area of the organ. Below it is the entire cerebrum, which entails the midbrain (limbic system), the brain stem (thalamus and recticular activating system), and the cerebellum (itself an almost separate "whole brain" in miniature).

A cursory glance at the brain and brain stem shows us that this system doesn't just stop; it continues on into that lengthy bundle of nerve fibers that run down our back, the spinal cord. Looking a bit closer, we see that various fibral networks run to and from the cord, and then we note an entire nervous system of fibers that connect up to every organ system of the body. So doing, we can now take our intellect/brain relationship into the realm of what we might describe as the "whole mind."

The point of the above outline is to illustrate that "intelligence" is not limited simply to left-brain rationalization, as exemplified by verbal and numerical prowess, but encompasses a far vaster organismic continuum. Our notion of intelligence must now take in the reality of the entire psyche itself, including personality, desire, and motivation, flexibility and willingness to learn, personal awareness, and creative potential. What we in the West must do now is to proceed to develop a much more holistic conception of intelligence, learning, and knowledge. Such a conceptual expansion may then lead to what can be referred to as a multi-IQ.

A multi-IQ would take in the total spectrum of intelligence, revealing whole-brain (instead of exclusively left-brain) comprehension, profiling various psychological, social, and perhaps even spiritual components. The pressing need for such an extradimensional appraisal of intelligence is underscored by Charles Tart in a penetrating article entitled "Some Assumptions of Orthodox, Western Psychology" (in *Transpersonal Psychologies*). In the subsection "Assumptions about Learning," he singles out four unproductive ideas about learning that need prompt attention. These include the assumptions that (1) learning is "nothing but" electrochemical changes in the nervous system; (2) learning is only a matter of accumulating knowledge; (3) intellectual learning is the highest form of learning, and high IQ is the only reliable gauge of one's potential to learn anything; and (4) learning is the process of taking in sensory impressions and processing them cognitively.[1]

Drawing primarily upon Eastern sources, Tart offers alternate viewpoints to those sketched above, which he sees as the major misconceptions about learning/intelligence in establishment psychology. His counterpoints are (1) learning cannot be theoretically reduced to electrochemical reactions in the brain or localized to specific areas therein; it may involve the entire psychophysical system, perhaps embracing those intangibles we denote as mind and consciousness, spirit and soul; (2) learning may be in large measure a result of *unlearning* and also have possible connections to subconscious, genetic/organic remembrance, or the activation of an innate collective unconscious (Jung); (3) intelligence and knowing may develop on a deeper level than the singular function we call intellect, via a balancing process of left- and right-brain faculties and the vertical functions as well, thus nurturing the growth of the greater psyche (mind, body, emotions, spirit); and (4) learning (increasing intelligence and knowledge) may be facilitated on an interior as well as an exterior plane(s), fostered in the "heart" as well as the head, in noncognitive, nonverbalized modes.

By enlarging our perspective on intelligence, our appreciation of our capacity to learn and grow will likewise be increased. We will better realize the full scope of our potential, much broader than what we unfortunately have been led to believe. Such an understanding, for most of us, can lead to a renewed self-confidence and motivation to explore, discover, learn, know, and do. Developed into its higher dimensions, intelligence is the outer expression of *being* itself, a state that lies beyond the concerns of day-to-day existence.

The implication of a multi-IQ for our educational system is long overdue and thus not actually "revolutionary." If indeed we humans have a multiplicity of potentials, then our schools and curricula (creations of our culture) are contributing to what might be called learned retardation by focusing on just a fraction of our overall capabilities. And this gross disservice does not always end in blissful ignorance; unfulfilled potential is undoubtedly the underrated cause of much emotional distress and mental illness (the fact that most Western societies are often described as neurotic by leading psychologists should not escape us in this regard).

David Elkind in "Misunderstandings about How Children Learn" clarifies the above assertions.[2] Elkind points out several commonplace and key misconceptions about children and how they learn and think. He cites many of the standardized "rules and regulations" as essentially hampering and unhealthy, yet part of the familiar folklore of disciplinary philosophy. For example, Elkind notes the old notion that children "learn best while sitting still and listening." The relatively recent mass diagnosis of "hyperactivity," primarily in boys, is interesting in this light.

Elkind emphasizes that play and action are crucially important in the child's learning processes and must be completely integrated into the schooling plan. Children do not seem to learn best in environments where there are too many rules, schedules, and inflexible programs. Nor is acceleration as important as elaboration (i.e., it can be harmful to rush certain children, the rush being more a reflection of our own impatience than concern for the child). Elaboration means giving children plenty of time to unfold and learn at their own innate pace and abundant diversity in their environment for exploring what they like and can excel at.

Elkind makes a number of other worthwhile observations on schooling, among them that many severe problems with children and education "could be avoided if concern for a child's achievements as a student were balanced by an equally strong concern for his feelings of self-worth as a person." He adds that the premium on strict intellectuality has devalued the personal-social facets of the individual in many other areas of society as well.

To take Elkind's (and other respected educational critics') evaluations a step further, it naturally follows that intellectual achievement, self-worth, and social value are not necessarily discrete, separate phenomena, but rather different aspects of the same whole-brain, whole-mind entity. The supposition rests on the realization that all areas of human growth and development are integrative and mutually dependent upon one another.

Notes

1. Charles T. Tart, "Some Assumptions of Orthodox Western Psychology," *Transpersonal Psychologies* (New York: Harper & Row, Publishers, 1975), pp. 100–102.
2. David Elkind, "Misunderstandings about How Children Learn," *Today's Education*, March 1972. Volume 61, No. 3, pp. 18–20.

Chapter Ten

Lifelong Learning

Learning is synonymous in the public mind with school, education with reading, writing, arithmetic, geography, and history. School itself is hardly distinguishable from industry, turning out long lines of uniformly informed human products. Education takes place on assembly lines of fact and within the walls of theory factories. Nothing else is serious education, is the common belief.

Nothing could be further from the truth. Whoever you are, wherever you are, learning and experience are at hand. You have only to reach out for it. With an open, receptive mind you can gather something here, something there.

> Take some substance from here to there ... You will make no profit if you go with empty hand.
>
> Khayyám[1]

Amongst all of the special characteristics of human beings, their infinite ability—but often latent motivation—to learn is their most fundamental. On this the sages of all time concur.

> A camel is stronger than a man; an elephant is larger; a lion has greater valour; cattle can eat more than man; birds are more virile. Man was made for the purpose of learning.
>
> Al Ghazzali[2]

Why is it then that so many people believe that receiving a diploma or certificate of achievement is a sign-off of learning, a license for resting on one's laurels? How has it come to be that knowledge is thought to be something that resides more in libraries and data banks than in the human mind itself? Actually, we all come into this world with almost unlimited possibilities, but unfortunately, for most people, few or none of their acorns of potential "into great oaks grow." Nature plans a unique curriculum for each of us, but we in the West do everything to thwart the plan. We begin life with what the brilliant educator Maria Montessori described as the "absorbent mind," only to have it plugged up by thickly jejune ideas and practices of parents, teachers and various other authorities who have no doubts about what they think education is. Says Montessori: "The education of our day is rich in methods, aims and social ends, but one must still say that it takes no account of life itself. . . . The world of education is like an island where people, cut off from the world, are prepared for life by exclusion from it."[3]

This training for mental insularity typifies the school sytem at all levels, from nursery school through university graduate school. Automatized brains are turned out in mass production, matriculating from lower to higher states of thought conformity all the way through. Once outside university walls, people are often at a loss to understand the problems and complexities of the world in which they find themselves.

Our entire philosophy of education is being increasingly called into question by many educators themselves, such as Montessori. The progressives among them believe that children have a much greater innate ability for teaching themselves than has heretofore been supposed. They see the teacher as a guide, someone who arranges conditions in the child's environment for optimal learning, stimulating exploration and experience. But the traditional teacher's role has been more or less the functional opposite of this: oversupervision, standing discipline (reward and punishment) and top-down arbitration. Students are made excessively dependent upon the teacher and are not trusted to teach themselves when possible. In addition, artificial aids are used too heavily, decreasing the psychological interface between teacher and student, depersonalizing a relationship that should be intensely personal.

Montessori calls this educational system "humiliating" and says that it "artificially lowers the powers of man. . . . It supplies men with crutches when they could run on swift feet." So we lurch out of school well conditioned to our crutches, thinking we have learned, and hobble through life so thoroughly programmed in this erroneous belief that we consistently fail to realize that learning, real learning, still awaits us. In *Reflections* Idries Shah observes:

> Man is a myth-maker.
>
> Myth, when manipulated by unregenerates, is an even more effective man-maker.
>
> Man (as he imagines himself to be), in general, is a possibility, not a fact.
>
> For most people, the sort of man whom they imagine to exist, or assume themselves to be, does not yet exist.[4]

Your real education, then, may be found not in school but elsewhere. One of the most implacable delusions of our modern culture is that what is taught formally is what is learned. Actually, the content (e.g., history, geography, math, English) is rarely retained. A few months, weeks, or even days after an exam, most students have forgotten almost everything they have memorized. Of course, a few ancillary skills will have been improved along the way: how to study, how to read better, how to take notes, how to cram for tests, how to snow instructors. Beyond these, however, what kinds of things of your own high school or college education do you remember? Chances are that instead of recalling what came out of books and teachers' mouths, you conjure up pictures and words of your old schoolmates, girlfriends/boyfriends, good times and bad times (exam times), attending ball games, sorority/fraternity parties, likable or lousy professors, sweating final grades, borrowing money from your parents to get through the term, and daily competition for a parking space.

The foregoing is not a wholesale advisement for quitting school or not enrolling. It does suggest a self-evaluation of one's need for classroom instruction beyond compulsory (grade and high school) education. And if you choose to be an astute dropout or stay-out, where else and what else can you learn while *not* in school? Probably the best reference on the subject is *The Lifelong Learner* by Ronald Gross.[5] In his opening Gross quotes Buckminster Fuller: "True higher learning is self-administered unlearning of most of what we've been taught in school." He then follows up with Stewart Brand, creator of the *Whole Earth Catalog*, who describes his occupation as "just goin' to school in the world." The lifelong learner extensively chronicles the numerous ways in which the world or life itself (the "invisible university") can teach us. And by education, Gross means far more than the academic connotations, defining it as "purposeful self-change." For this task you don't need certificates or degrees.

What are the signs of "purposeful change," the proof, in fact, that true learning has taken place? According to Gross, they are "accomplishments, capabilities, social effects, strengthened sensitivities and convictions—in such consequences is free learning properly measured." The "invisible university" or "college in your head" is virtually everywhere, wherever there is a source of free learning. Libraries, museums, zoos, movies, some television, social and professional organizations, community services of various kinds, and "learning exchanges" are but a few open formats for hands-on and brains-on learning. Even most colleges and universities are (albeit too slowly) beginning to realize the limitations of high-cost pass/fail education and offer, often for a modest fee, noncredit courses, taught by nonprofessors on evenings and weekends. These classes usually emphasize practicality, field work, and interpersonal activity. You can learn how to tune up your car, grow a vegetable garden, weave a rug, manage your stress, invest your money, assert yourself creatively. Also, there are university-affiliated (or private) seminars and workshops on many important and interesting topics such as self-care (mental and physical), creativity, educating both sides of your brain, living the single life, and sexual adjustment.

But education does not stop with specialized instruction. Each and every "life experience" can teach us something of value. These can be major or minor events, planned or unplanned—it doesn't matter. Just sitting under a tree and watching an ant hill can be enlightening. Working through some serious or difficult situation is a kind of psychic alchemy that can leave us with much more wisdom than we had before. Marriage, parenthood, foreign travel, a business venture, or even an acute illness or other misfortune may call upon mental and spiritual resources previously dormant. Then there are all the people and places just around the corner we tend to take so much for granted—a factory, a farm, an auto-repair shop, a psychologist, a dentist (yes, you can learn even in the chair), a newspaper office, theatres, television stations, a telephone repairperson. The "invisible university" is something you cast your eyes upon many times a day without seeing. Everyone and everything has something to offer us that we can learn from. Dreams can teach us a good deal, as can books (but of course), television shows (try to be an open-minded critic here), theatrical productions. If you live in a small community, the range of such contacts will naturally be more limited—nonetheless, the opportunities are there in one form or another, and you have only to open your eyes to them.

Of all learning environments, nature itself is surely the most underrated. Animals, plants, trees, landscapes, lakes, meadows, forests, rivers, oceans, deserts, mountains, the sky—as a teacher, nature is a ubiquitous sage. Here is where aspiring students of life outside large cities have the advantage. Yet in megalopolises are to be found parks, lagoons, flower and botanical gardens, bird sanctuaries, and various places where you can see animals and fish (zoos, pet shops). In some cities (usually on the outskirts) you can make a trip to an observatory/

planetarium and have your mind expanded just by being on the premises. You may be lucky enough to get a peek through a telescope, but if not, you will probably be afforded a bird's-eye view of your locale, if the facility is on an elevated site, as is usual.

> Speak to the earth, and it shall teach thee. . . .
> Job 12:8

> Siddhartha said: "Is it not true, my friend, that the river has very many voices? Has it not the voice of a king, of a warrior, of a bull, of a night bird, of a pregnant woman and a sighing man, and a thousand other voices?"
>
> "It is so," nodded Vasudeya, "the voices of all living creatures are in its voice."
> Herman Hesse

Each of us can be, like Zorba the Greek, a relishing learner of life. But some of us are better learners than others. How can we improve our learning capacity? First, and above all, we must *value* understanding and knowledge for themselves. We must really *understand* the importance of learning and proceed to cultivate the *desire* to learn. You may have to remember initially that as children we were naturally curious about the world around us, and asked questions in never-ending wonderment, but this healthy proclivity was discouraged and schooled out of us. As adults, having gone through the conditioning processes described in chapter 3, we have had our curiosity blunted and our questions muted.

Next, we need to *unlearn*—to unlearn the notion that knowledge is something found only in schools and libraries, that only experts have it, and that "learning" is accumulating second-hand, and often trivial, facts. To become learners we must hone our basic endowments (perception, intuition, cognition) and learning skills. We must practice listening beyond mere hearing and observing beyond mere seeing, and we must read in depth. Most of us have as yet little capacity to really pay attention and absorb, despite the harangues we received as children for not doing so ("pay attention to what?"). We need to relearn how to ask questions, in order to prompt honest and undiluted answers. And to answer in this mode also.

Those are our most human skills, but they are corroded by nonuse, like artifacts in a sand dune. The corrosive elements we must neutralize are such habits as arrogance, narcissism (the ability to relinquish attention upon oneself), and egocentricity. Hidden biases must be uncovered, thinking liberalized, prejudices challenged. Taking interest in widely divergent phenomena helps give one deeper perspective on everything. The making of a political candidate may seem on the surface to have no similarity to the evolution of a scientific theory, but there are some shared dynamics. To be an astute observer, to absorb all that is going on around you, you must become present centered. Forget yesterday and tomorrow when you are trying to concentrate on the moment. Slow down. Consider everything around you are interrelated (including yourself) and significant in some way, be it dramatic or not. An excellent source book on observation, discovery, and situation consciousness is Edward deBono's *Learn To Think*.[6] The book contains a wealth of material on thinking and perceiving in new ways, with strategies on how to become more flexible and open.

Reading is an abundantly accessible channel to knowledge, but you must be selective about books, periodicals, and all printed matter; there is so much of it, running a gamut of quality from atrocious to transcendent. Begin by just reading books that interest you, that turn you on. Less TV may be in order for you to have more reading time. After you are reading more avidly, begin delving into things that are largely unfamiliar to you that still might interest you. If you have immersed yourself in novels in the past, turn to nonfiction. Once more, remember that good reading is like good eating: quality counts, not quantity. Rumination, digestion, and absorption are aided by relaxation. If you have trouble concentrating, perhaps you are under too much anxiety or stress, in which case certain kinds of pastoral or spiritual literature can be of some help.

The importance of continuing learning, of open-mindedness and psychic growth is trenchantly put by the astute thinker and teacher Krishnamurti:

> Since you are young, fresh, innocent, can you look at all the beauty of the earth, have the quality of affection? And can you retain that? For if you do not, as you grow up, you will conform, because that is the easiest way to live. . . . You have to change society, but not by killing people. Society is you and I. You and I create the society in which we live. So you have to change.[7]

This excerpt is from Krishnamurti's book *On Education*. He defines education as self-change rather than schooling. He asks the poignant question: "What is the point of your passing examinations, getting a job and settling down in life as millions and millions of people do? . . . Is that the meaning of education?" He then goes on to explain, quite correctly, that the purpose of formal schooling, everywhere in the world, is to be educated to conform, to "fit" into one's culture and society, "to be sucked into that vast stream that has been flowing for thousands of years."

We agree with Krishnamurti that *real* education should have the polarly *opposite* function—to teach us how not to be sucked in, how not to conform, to learn how to think for ourselves and make our minds our own.

Notes

1. Idries Shah, *The Way of the Sufi*. New York: Dutton, 1970, p. 60.
2. Ibid., p. 57.
3. Maria Montessori, *The Absorbent Mind* (New York: Dell, 1967), pp. 20–21.
4. Idries Shah, *Reflections* (Baltimore: Penguin Books, 1972), p. 59.
5. Ronald Gross, *The Lifelong Learner* (New York: Simon and Schuster, 1977).
6. Edward deBono and De Saint-Arnaud, Michael. *Learn To Think* (Santa Barbara, Calif.: Capra Press, 1982).
7. J. Krishnamurti, *On Education* (New York: Harper & Row, Publishers, 1974), pp. 15–17.

Chapter Eleven

Learning How to Learn

For the inordinate amount of time and energy contemporary psychology (from 1900 to the present) has devoted to the mechanics of conditioning, precious little has been found out about human learning itself, beyond a handful of pointers on how to study. Here the emphasis is on memory and recall, an outgrowth of the research, as you may remember, in Pavlovian (associational) and operant (trial-and-error) conditioning. Behavioral psychology has been fixated upon these principles ever since. So the measure of learning has been taken as the amount of units of any information that is correctly memorized and recalled. Under the heading "Aids in Learning" in a modern introductory text (*Psychology: An Introduction* by Charles G. Morris) are listed the main factors that research psychologists have determined affect the learning process: study time (the more time spent studying the better), distribution of practice (take rest breaks in between), speeded reading (if you read too fast, absorption will decrease), arousal level (very high arousal or anxiety or very low arousal can reduce retention and recall), effects of sleep (retention is best if you study before sleeping), knowledge of results (feedback improves performance), and whole versus part learning (it's easier to learn by organizing the material into a meaningful whole than bit by bit).[1]

As an example of the last factor, two word lists are shown:

- North, man, red, spring, woman, east, autumn, yellow, summer, boy, blue, west, winter, girl, green, south.
- North, east, south, west, spring, summer, autumn, winter, red, yellow, green, blue, man, woman, boy, girl.

Guess which list is easier to learn and remember (not exactly a brainstrainer).

The bulk of the research on the subject of human learning has been quite trivial and circumscribed. The overriding emphasis has been on word/concept memory, not "learning" as meant in the larger context of that term. Whether spewing out correct answers on command can even be defined as having learned in any higher context is also open to question. If so, it is a most elementary form, the rudiments observed in trained parrots. The revelations of over a century of psychological studies have been limited to a few passing eye openers, which should have been evident to "common sense" anyway. By trying too hard to be scientific, to conduct "pure" research with humans, to keep their methods and concepts as simple as possible, the psychological specialists have ended up with reams and reams of "simple" findings that do not tell much at all, despite all of the tedious tests, statistics, replications, parameters, and controls.

Given the above, the idea of "learning how to learn" (as distinguished from learning how to memorize) has been rare, if not virtually unknown, in psychology. This process entails the increasing of a certain *capacity* to integrate each successive learning experience into a greater synthesis of comprehension and understanding, beyond the random associational (of Pavlovian conditioning) and trial-and-error (operant conditioning) modes. Real learning, as opposed to these latter, transcends the limits of conditioning, and in so doing results in understanding and knowledge. The difference is qualitative; any animal can be conditioned, including the human, but not all humans can learn, in this higher sense, in their present state.

Because experimental psychology has focused on observables only, mentalistic concepts such as perception, intuition, and illumination have been shunted aside as unquantifiable notions. Instead, the parameters of performance alone are the main foci of study, taking precedence over all other considerations, even the concept of mind itself. One of the rare notable exceptions to this one-track research was a series of monkey experiments carried out by Harry F. Harlow in the late 1940s. In these experiments the monkeys were first trained to discriminate between differently shaped objects (e.g., between squares and circles) in order to get food (placed under one block figure and not another). After accomplishing this task, they were given a new choice situation (e.g., triangles versus rectangles). They learned this second discrimination more quickly. After a time the animals were capable of performing a new two-choice task quite rapidly, with just a few tries.

According to Harlow, when a monkey or any animal masters a series of such tasks in progressively efficient fashion, it has learned a general principle or acquired a "learning set." Since the organism had to go through preliminary experiences, had to gain insight into a general principle before it could perform faster and more easily on later tasks, Harlow reasoned that it had learned how to learn. Modern psychology, in its slow move from pure behavioral to cognitive behavioral theory and experiment, has referred to such results as Harlow's as *cognitive learning*—apparently a bold move for scientific psychologists, since the implication is that something insightful, and hence mental, is going on.

Learning how to learn as the avenue to advanced knowledge and self-understanding was introduced to psychology through the back door, so to speak, by someone outside the official fold—namely a modern sage, Idries Shah. Though his ideas were intimated in his earlier works, dating from 1964, it was his 1978 book, *Learning How to Learn*, that fully outlined his thinking on the subject. His concepts were then amplified in two later works, *A Perfumed Scorpion* (also in 1978) and *Seeker after Truth* (1982).[2] Among many related topics, Shah delineates specific and numerous social conditions in the West (and East) that act as barriers and conductors of learning.

Shah's emphasis is on *capacity* and those factors that facilitate a state of mind capable of the deep absorption of experience and true learning. "To learn" by his definition is, to repeat, to gain greater understanding through the experience of what is familiarly called the human condition. "Learning how" to do this entails the study of particular mechanisms of conditioning (primarily emotive and cognitive) that are observable in oneself and the society at large. The capacity for learning how to learn depends upon a stabilized intensification of awareness in proper alignment with purpose and volition. This enterprise is typically undertaken in a context of existential significance. Conditioning, on the other hand, in its many forms usually happens outside conscious recognition, demands but a minimal level of awareness, is often involuntary, is frequently used for mental manipulation, and not infrequently pertains to superficial matters.

Because of the format and general thrust of his writings, Shah does not set off learning against conditioning. The latter, however, is consistently stressed (sometimes as automatism) by him implicitly as those ubiquitous social and personal elements that prevent one from learning. To be a good learner, it would seem, involves the opposite propensities of one who is easily conditioned or manipulated. Learning how to learn is not a light undertaking and often takes years of sustained personal effort. This effort must be regularly reoriented; otherwise it is similar to trying to sail a ship to a distant port without basic navigation. Thinking that such a skill can be acquired on a random, pick-and-choose basis without unnecessary waste of time and energy and risk of loss (beyond time and energy) generally identifies one as unpromising for the task. Initial guidance can come from reading Shah's revolutionary books and reflecting thoroughly upon the principles set out there, for they clearly encompass the various facets of the orientation. But Shah implies also that reading itself may eventually not be enough, as additional, personalized assistance is commonly necessary.

It follows, from all that has been discussed thus far, that clearing the mind of the dross of conditioning is essentially an operation of *unlearning*. Consciousness must be emptied of all the debris that impairs perception and cognition. A classical Zen tale illustrates this principle: A disciple wants to learn and approaches his master with this aim. The latter, without a word, pours tea from a kettle into the disciple's cup. The disciple observing, the master continues pouring the tea, the cup overflowing. The disciple is momentarily baffled and questions the efficacy of this action, but the master suggests he think it out. In due course the disciple realizes that before he can learn anything of value he must first empty his mind of unneeded ideas, concepts, thoughts, and habits—the "overflow" of useless content. "You must pour out the dirty water before you pour in the clean," echoes a Sufi maxim.

Unlearning or emptying of the mind cannot be accomplished on a time scale, nor by some simple technique, such as meditation. While various gurus and spiritual hucksters may try to convince us otherwise (taking our money in the process), such "Eastern" pastimes as meditation, yoga postures, or breathing exercises are *not* the means of achieving permanently cleared consciousness. At best, these random, piecemeal exercises are capable of providing some momentary relaxation and stress reduction, nothing much more. Reports by endless scores of students that such techniques have "changed my life" or "given me spiritual bliss" are more reflective of their own naiveté, gullibility, and oversuggestibility than anything else. It is not that these kinds of practices can have no function in learning how to learn, but they may or may not be indicated at any point in study. Genuine exercises are temporary aids, and not prescribed indiscriminately for anyone at any time. In authentic schools they are performed within a broad context of instruction and nonexotic learning experiences.

In Sufi schools, for example, where levels of instruction become most sophisticated and advanced, the program of studies projected from a teaching center can be of such a type that students acquire certain skills, like those discussed above, without ever being directly taught those skills. The ability, for instance, to enter into a state of deep contemplation may be developed epiphenomenally, as the result of correct application of general principles of an overtly unrelated sort. This subtle method is common to Sufism, which holds that some lessons can be learned only indirectly. The concept is baffling to many externalists whose lack of understanding of it leads them to believe that it is mystification.

Teaching and learning through indirect means is portrayed in the following story, which illustrates how the method may be used to overcome negative proclivities in the student.

THE PARABLE OF THE GREEDY SONS

There was once a hard-working and generous farmer who had several idle and greedy sons. On his deathbed he told them that they would find his treasure if they were to dig in a certain field. As soon as the old man was dead, the sons hurried to the fields, which they dug up from one end to another, and with increasing desperation and concentration when they did not find the gold in the place indicated.

But they found no gold at all. Realizing that in his generosity their father must have given his gold away in his lifetime, they abandoned the search. Finally, it occurred to them that, since the land had been prepared, they might as well sow a crop. They planted wheat, which produced an abundant yield. They sold this crop and prospered that year.

After the harvest was in, the sons thought again about the bare possibility that they might have missed the buried gold, so they again dug up their fields, with the same result.

After several years they became accustomed to labour, and to the cycle of the seasons, something which they had not understood before. Now they understood the reason for their father's method of training them, and they became honest and contented farmers. Ultimately they found themselves possessed of sufficient wealth no longer to wonder about the hidden hoard.

Thus it is with the teaching of understanding of human destiny and the meaning of life. The teacher, faced with impatience, confusion and covetousness on the part of the students, must direct them to an activity which is known by him to be constructive and beneficial to them, but whose true function and aim is often hidden from them by their own rawness.

Accompanying the parable is Shah's commentary:

> This story, underlining the claim that a person may develop certain faculties in spite of his attempts to develop others, is unusually widely known. This may be because it carries the preface, "Those who repeat it will gain more than they know."
>
> It was published both by the Franciscan Roger Bacon (who quotes the Sufi philosophy and taught at Oxford, from which he was expelled by order of the Pope) and the seventeenth-century chemist Boerhaave.
>
> This version is attributed to the Sufi, Hasan of Basra, who lived nearly twelve-hundred years ago.[3]

Characteristics that mitigate against ease of learning are many of those signified by that homely heading "Human Nature." These are the major barriers preventing the permanent learning of designed or undesigned lessons. A true teacher knows what kind of a lesson the student needs, based on the idiosyncrasies of the latter's "human nature" and his or her aptitude for perception and absorption of meaning. Greed, anger, conceit, vanity, arrogance, egocentricity, selfishness, and the like must be overcome by would-be learners. Naturally they cannot do so simply because they want to. There are many reasons for this, and most of them are "I" problems. That is, there are many conflicting "I's" or personalities inside each of us. So while one part of us wants to remove negative qualities from this unharmonious crowd, a slew of other pseudo-selves continually work against this end. The personality that desires positive change is the real self, but without circumstances (learning situations at opportune times) conducive to its growth and strength, it cannot gain control of the sabotaging "I's."

Usually, attempting to gain the upper hand over negative tendencies by sheer will power falls far short of success. A battle may be won here and there, but for the most part there exists no controlling "I" to maintain order amongst the various warring factions of the personality. A more effective strategy, one infinitely more harmonious and less exhausting, is to gradually transform and harness negative energies for ultimately positive ends. Something like this energy conversion is found in the Freudian hypothesis of sublimation, where the sexual drive is rechanneled into creative pursuits such as art or dance. Yet this is simply redirection, and actual transformation might require much more sophisticated expertise and technique.

Those who have established a unitary "I" and are capable of teaching others to achieve the same thing are themselves the products of a system that minimizes the waste of energy and time. On one's own, the enterprise of self-development may take a lifetime of trial and error, with no odds-on for success. The machinations of the ego (the complex of false selves) undermine objective appraisal at nearly every turn. The neutralization of the ego is part and parcel of the difficult phase of preparation, of learning to learn. Venturing on this formidable task is risky and has frequently proven harmful, especially when the sense of self is not inherently strong.

It should be understood that the teacher-student relationship in this context bears no similarity to authoritarian systems, as exemplified in classroom education. Nor is it akin to the benign manipulation of the typical guru-disciple tryst. The student must make his or her own efforts, must help himself or herself, and make progress on his or her own. Perhaps the interaction is more parallel to that of doctor and patient; the former guides and prescribes, but the latter must take responsibility for his or her own well-being. The teacher helps students to help themselves.

"Back to basics" is the plea that has been resounding recently from parents whose children are failing to learn essential academic skills in school. The implication is that not enough *time* is being alloted to these skills. But perhaps time is not the problem—instead, *method*. Reading, writing, and arithmetic are forced upon all students, on uniform schedules. Yet some students are more ready than others to acquire certain abilities at a given time. When the latter have trouble learning, they are given lower grades or "held back," thereby made to feel like underachievers. In addition, most subjects are taught by rote demonstration, although many children learn more efficiently by experimentation and quiet guidance—that is to say, more *indirectly.*

Marilyn Ferguson (*The Aquarian Conspiracy*) believes that we should indeed get back to basics, but by this she means learning how to think and learning the "bedrock fundamentals" involved in the process. There are many "illiterates" around the world who are yet superior thinkers—so perhaps the problems do not really begin with ineptitude in literacy but are evidence of a more fundamental shortcoming in our schooling system. It is Ferguson's position that students must learn the underlying principles and relationships of real, "universal" education. Hence, prior to or coterminous with academic training, students should learn experience *outside* the classroom. "Freedom, high expectations, awareness, patterns, connections, creativity" are the "basics" she sees as missing.[4]

A new preparatory or supplemental curriculum, as suggested by Ferguson, would teach pupils such elementary self-knowledge as personal psychology, managing stress (and do kids need that!), social skills, independence (not selfish insulation), and most of all, how to think. Despite the fact that thinking is one of our most important faculties, few schools offer courses exclusively designed for this "basic." As to discipline (highly touted by back-to-basics fundamentalists), why not assist students early on to maintain internal control, preferable by far to stick-and-carrot approaches? Internally derived discipline could be taught by using such developmental tools as relaxation techniques, breathing exercises, and self-understanding.

An idea of how such a basic-maintenance curriculum might be designed is offered up by Tony Buzan in his *Use Both Sides of Your Brain.* He posits a model that is more "organic" and person centered (instead of subject centered), osmotic, and spontaneous. Instead of dispersing impersonal information wholesale to students, in the hope of their swallowing and digesting it, Buzan's system would first teach students about themselves and impart to them practical methods with which to improve their recall, creativity, thinking and problem-solving skills. To bolster these rudimentary abilities, they would then learn how to read better, listen, take notes (Buzan has devised an innovative note-taking technique), write expressively, and so on. All of this, according to Buzan, would "make teaching and learning much easier, more enjoyable and more productive." In other words, the harmony and balance between the teacher, the subject matter and the student will have been restored.[5]

Because the concept of learning how to learn is an alien one to most people, educational philosophies such as Ferguson's and Buzan's are sure to meet initial resistance. However, the purpose and necessity of such revision is urgent indeed. The very automatic rejection of new ideas is itself a sure sign that there is something amiss in many people's thinking. We tend to see and hear only that which we *want* to see and hear, which is usually those platitudes and pseudo-truths flattering to our biases. It isn't always enough just to point something out to people and expect them to believe it. Other factors have to be taken into account and dealt with before the "message" can be effectively delivered. So it is with all learning.

This brings up a collateral principle of learning: *registration*. We could say that this function too is a mental faculty. Before information can be absorbed, it must first be fully registered. As an easily distracted species, we are inclined to "take in" things much too casually and rapidly (especially in fast-paced environments today), so much so that the subtleties, the covert content of information and experience, are lost. This propensity is amplified by a general lack of awareness, the habit of being too superficial in all of our activities. Of this human weakness a great sage, Abdullah Faroz, speaks:

Read this again and again until you understand it, register it.

As it turns out, Abdullah Faroz is fictitious; the quotation may seem to mean something if the nonsense itself doesn't sink in.

That's how a lot of gobbledygook and subtle information alike get past us if we listen or read shallowly.

Now let's try for some insight into the problem at hand. Here are "Three Pieces of Advice" from Rumi's classic, *The Masnavi*.

THREE PIECES OF ADVICE

A man once caught a bird. The bird said to him, "I am no use to you as a captive. But let me free, and I will tell you three valuable pieces of advice."

The bird promised to give the first piece of advice while still in the man's grasp, the second when he reached a branch, the third after he had gained the top of a mountain.

The man agreed, and asked for the first piece of advice.

The bird said:

"If you lose something, even if it be valued by you as much as life itself—do not regret it."

Now the man let the bird go, and it hopped to a branch.

It continued with the second piece of advice:

"Never believe anything which is contrary to sense, without proof."

Then the bird flew to the mountain-top. From here it said:

"O unfortunate one! Within me are two huge jewels, and if you had only killed me they would have been yours!"

The man was anguished at the thought of what he had lost, but he said: "At least now tell me the third piece of advice."

The bird replied:

"What a fool you are, asking for more advice when you have not given thought to the first two pieces! I told you not to worry about what had been lost, and not to believe in something contrary to sense. Now you are doing both. You are believing something ridiculous and grieving because you have lost something! I am not big enough to have inside of me huge jewels.

"You are a fool. Therefore you must stay within the usual restrictions imposed on man."

In dervish circles, this tale is regarded as of very great importance in "sensitizing" the mind of the student, preparing it for experiences which cannot be elicited in ordinary ways.

In addition to being in daily use among Sufis, the story is found in the Rumi classic, the *Mathnavi*. It is featured in the *Divine Book* of Attar, one of the teachers of Rumi. Both men lived in the thirteenth century.[6]

So Rumi gave us, over seven hundred years ago, a good reason why back to basics is essentially a sham today. To simply learn how to read and write (assuming the B-to-B'rs have the method) is just not enough. The mechanics of these skills are next to useless without more basic mental equipment. Would-be learners must learn about themselves, about why they think or do not think as they do, about selective perception. This personal exploration can start quite early in life, yet it is virtually nonexistent in today's education.

Take a look at the five cards in Figure 11-1. Count the total number of clubs on each card. Are there ten per card? (Do it!)

Did you notice anything besides the number of clubs? Perhaps that there are some mistakes in areas other than the club-counting task requested of you? Would you believe it if you were told that only one of the five cards is printed correctly? Check again.[7]

Now describe what you see in the shape in Figure 11-2.

Figure 11-1.

Figure 11-2.

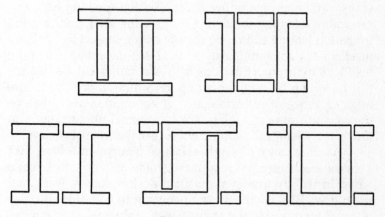

Figure 11-3.

Most people give only one description. If your mind is more flexible than the average, you perceived more than one (and possibly several) images in the shape. A few of these possibilities are provided in Figure 11-3.[8]

These visual possibilities, interpreted in Figure 11-3 in terms of bare relationships, are by no means exhaustive. Other contexts exist—hence the form might be described as a section of a horizontal ladder or as two Siamese letter Ts on a bar, and so on. The ability to see matters in alternative perspectives, to have an open and flexible mind, is not something we are encouraged or taught to develop. On the contrary, in school we are trained to believe that there is only one correct answer to a given problem. Our obsession with tests and exams tends to reinforce this "one right answer" trap.

Vanity, pride, and defense mechanisms may seem to have little to do with the dynamics of such exercises as we have just given, yet they play an important part in limiting perception in the larger fields of life. Defense mechanisms, as Sigmund Freud noted, are deeply concealed mental acts of denial, which are stronger proportionately as they are believed, cherished, and defended by the "victim," who does not recognize their maleficent effects. Defense mechanisms can be simple or elaborate—it doesn't matter. There are several generic forms, with many variations, including rationalization (making excuses), projection (blaming someone or something else), and reaction formation (acting and doing the opposite). In essence, defense mechanisms are nothing more than self-deception and false justification for something one has done, failed to do, or merely thinks, which he cannot own up to in himself or anyone else because of fear of embarrassment or humiliation. Nonetheless, the unworthiness of saving face is summed up succinctly in the saying, "Self-justification is worse than the original offense."[9]

Another cause of overly selective perception is bias. Like defense mechanisms it may masquerade as rationality, while based in wholly irrational personal desires, hopes, fears, and prejudices. Bias manifests as a penchant to take sides, to play up one's (or one's interest group's) own "rightness" over another, different position. It is loading intellectual dice to discredit an opposing point of view. Few people are immune, as practitioners or recipients. Newspapers are shot through with evidence of all kinds of bias. The editorial pages brim over with it. Even textbooks, which we assume are objective, are replete with slanted perspectives and misemphases. American history books are so different from their Russian counterparts, for example, that one is tempted to think that political impartiality is a lost cause, at least among published historians. Science textbooks also contain hidden bias. For example, where American pyschology texts emphasize, say, behavioral principles, many of those published in Austria are heavily loaded with psychoanalytic concepts.

Many vegetarians believe that eating meat is unhealthy for the body and makes one aggressive (there is no experimental proof of this). Their ideas would no doubt seem bizarre to members of a certain robust African tribe who subsist on nothing but milk and beef. Presidents of the United States have convinced themselves and others that spending $200 billion a year on weapons is justified to stem the menacing "Red tide," while the leaders of the USSR up the armaments ante on their side because of "American imperialism." On the largest scale we see the pot calling the kettle black.

As can be seen everywhere, there is much mental silt stopping up the human brain, preventing the full flow of perceptive thought necessary for learning how to learn. Recognizing the problem and acknowledging the need for a program in learning readiness, however, does not mean that one possesses the ability to design such a program, should he or she desire. Our knowledge here is limited, simply because it is so new to us. Undoubtedly, psychologists and educators will increasingly focus on the phenomenon of capacity, how learning is learnt, for some time to come. The endeavor should benefit us all.

Notes

1. Charles G. Morris, *Psychology: An Introduction* (Englewood Cliffs, N.J.: Prentice-Hall, 1976), p. 195.
2. Idries Shah, *Learning How To Learn: Psychology and Spirituality in The Sufi Way* (San Francisco: Harper & Row, Publishers, 1978); *A Perfumed Scorpion* (San Francisco: Harper & Row, Publishers, 1978); *Seeker After Truth* (London: Octagon Press, 1982).
3. Idries Shah, *Tales of The Dervishes* (New York: E. P. Dutton & Co., 1970), pp. 144–45.
4. Marilyn Ferguson, *The Aquarian Conspiracy* (Los Angeles: J. P. Tarcher, 1980).
5. Tony Buzan, *Use Both Sides of Your Brain* (New York: E. P. Dutton & Co., 1976).
6. Shah, *Tales of The Dervishes*, pp. 132–33.
7. Idries Shah, *The Way of the Sufi*. New York: Dutton, 1970, p. 139.
8. From *The Book of Modern Puzzles* by Gerald L. Kaufman, Dover Publications, Inc., New York, 1954. Reprinted through permission of the publisher.
9. Figure 1-6 of *New Think* by Edward deBono. © 1967, 1968 by Edward deBono, Basic Books, Inc., Publishers, New York. Reprinted

with permission of the publisher and Edward deBono, author of *The Mechanism of Mind* (Simon & Schuster), *Lateral Thinking for Management* (American Management Association), and *Beyond Yes and No* (Simon & Schuster).

10. From The Book of Modern Puzzles by Gerald L. Kaufman, Dover Publications Inc., New York, 1954. Reprinted through permission of the Publisher.

11. Figures 11-2 and 11-3 of *New Think* by Edward de Bono. © 1967, 1968 by Edward de Bono, Basic Books, Inc., Publishers, New York. Reprinted with permission of the publisher and Edward de Bono, author of the *Mechanism of Mind* (Simon & Schuster), *Lateral Thinking for Management* (American Management Association), and *Beyond Yes and No* (Simon & Schuster).

Chapter Twelve
Knowledge and Wisdom

As we begin to reach higher thresholds of mental capacity, accompanied by an expansion of personal fulfillment and freedom, a curious thing happens regularly. Hitting temporary limits, it is not unusual to feel somewhat frustrated at the inability to accelerate further. For us whose pace is more tortoise style than harelike the letdown is the mere feeling of having lost our "roll"; the tortoise seems to be sitting still. Not a welcome sensation after a good start off and running for the gold. This letdown is due in large part to the typical Western trait of hyperimpatience. The best remedy is simply to remember that speed is not relevant on this journey. The journey itself takes precedence, and sometimes one needs to rest and take stock.

In the foregoing pages you should have picked up, through explication or implication, useful pointers for learning how to tune up your mental engine and fuel it with cognitive energy so that it can be "driven" in an efficient, flexible, and controlled manner. Most of us are as yet inexpert drivers. Yet the question remains: Where is this wondrous vehicle, the mind/brain, ultimately going to take us? The answer cannot just be given to the individual traveler on the path of self-development, which takes place progressively as she or he reaches the higher ground of knowledge and wisdom.

In considering wisdom itself, we must distinguish between the first-hand learning that culminates in it and the second-hand programmed knowledge that does not, however intellectually valid. This crucial distinction has been propounded in various contexts throughout this book. For reasons that have been discussed, it is not one easily absorbed by many people. In humans mental conditioning pertains primarily to indoctrination, the inculcation of beliefs and opinions that later manifest from subconscious levels as assumptions, thought by the indoctrinated to be unquestionable truths. Like conditioning, experiential learning is transacted in the brain, but otherwise the two are as different as close-order drill and improvisational mime.

"Education is an admirable thing," actress Katharine Hepburn once remarked, "but it is well to remember from time to time that nothing that is worth knowing can be taught." We can assume she is talking about rote instruction rather than skillful demonstration. The latter method, for instance, is undoubtedly the best for teaching someone how to plant and cultivate a beautiful flower garden, while the former may not even enable one to prepare the soil properly. Our cerebral soil likewise is not tilled adequately by modern educational systems. The crux of this problem was summed up several millenia ago by the Greek philosopher Epictetus: "What concerns me is not the way things are but rather the way people think things are." Too many of today's educators seem disinclined to be bothered about either condition.

In referring to knowledge, we should comprehend that it has ascending gradations, or levels. Ordinary people have access to three basic categories of knowledge, increasingly difficult in progression. They are as follows:

- *Common knowledge:* The world of everyday experience, given consensual meaning by the larger culture: riding a bicycle; "The sky is blue, I love you."

- *Conceptual knowledge:* The intellectual, logical mode, common to science. Rationality subordinates the sensual experience of common knowledge. Explains in theory why the sky is blue.

- *Higher knowledge:* Like common knowledge, based in experience, but unlike it, involves the reality beyond sensate experience. Is independent of conceptual knowledge and cannot be verified by it.

Higher knowledge is of an entirely different order of learning than common and conceptual knowledge, in that it is not conditioned into the mind by automatic processes. Rather it is organically activated within the mind by direct perception. The knowledge so gained by this primally personal method is truly the individual's own, as contrasted to conceptual knowledge which, though valid for its own purposes, cannot encompass the vaster realities beyond terrestrially limited measurement and language.

Knowledge and wisdom are rare. Much of what passes for them is merely coalesced pseudo-certainty. Insight, realization, understanding, and wisdom are the products of experience. And right experience at that. They are qualities that, when nurtured properly, develop coextensively with natural evolution. They are the channels to the "external verities." The ineffable reality and truth to which they lead are most difficult to express in words. Prose, poetry, and other of the finest works of art are only reflections.

Higher knowledge often relates to scientific fact, but the latter, dealing with concrete phenomena, is basically changeable (as technology improves to revise "facts"). Real (higher) knowledge is absolute and takes in self-knowledge, life, and the cosmos. It is that which we associate with the most advanced wise men such as Jesus, Buddha, Mohammed, Moses, Lao-Tse, and Confucius. Wisdom is not learned in the same way as, say, morality is learned in Sunday School. It cannot be imparted by advice or rule but is gained through good counsel, correct perception, and right action. Wisdom accumulates in everyday life and existence, arriving through the "heart" as well as the head. It requires a quite different kind of "homework" than reading textbooks and writing themes. Out in the workaday world we can clarify this qualitative contrast by comparing, as but one example among many, a psychology professor and a clinical psychologist. The professor may have never had a real patient in her life, yet is nonetheless respected, even revered for her formidable book knowledge. On the other hand, the clinician not only is usually well read but has a firsthand working knowledge of emotional pathology as well. Haven't we all known someone who can trot out an intellectual harangue as perfectly as a champion show horse in dressage, but when it comes to human relations or practical matters, well, performs as though he or she has seldom been out of the stall?

Which brings us back again to the recurring human frailty of underdeveloped perception and judging by appearances. "If he looks good, he *is* good" is a bit of wit capsulizing the mind that is impressed with the externals of performance, propriety, and piety. Somehow we think that observable sanctity must always accompany great wisdom and spirituality. When this belief takes too strong a hold on, for instance, community religion, the effects can be dynamically interesting—and always undesirable. The folk tale is a pointed example. The setting is the Middle East, but the type is to be found everywhere.

RHEUMATISM AND RELIGION

A stranger of apparently advanced age entered a mosque one Friday and engaged in his prayers at such length and exertion that the other worshippers thought he must be a pious man indeed. In time, this man was looked upon as a paragon of devotion to Allah. His example stirred his fellow suppliants to redouble their ritual fervor. Several even tried to keep their foreheads to their prayer rug longer than the newcomer, who always kept to himself and resided, with his wife, on the outside of town.

One day one of these admirers saw the "venerable one" struggling up onto a donkey backwards. "Perhaps this is an acting out of some deep teaching, staged for my benefit," he thought.

At that moment some neighborhood urchins rollicked by, laughing and hooting at what was clearly an ass on an ass. To the observer's high surprise, the latter shook his fist and swore at the rowdies with such vehemence that the animal was started, carrying him off unceremoniously. At the commotion a woman had emerged from the nearby house and now stood looking at the puffs of dust.

The mosque-goer approached her uncertainly and queried, "Is not that man gone yonder on the donkey a holy sage?"

"Not unless he has lived a secret life from me these twenty years," she answered. "That is my husband, Salman."

"But do you not know that he is unequaled in time spent in prostration at our mosque? And when he rises, it is with such signs of untold suffering as have not been witnessed by any of us. And when he intones the name of Allah it is as if his very breath were taken away."

"That would be his emphysema," said the wife, "brought on by many years of heavy cigarette smoking, a habit he acquired abroad. As for his groans, that is the voice of his aching back, complaining yet from too many years hunched over the gaming tables."

Aghast, the questioner persisted, "But surely it is his latent wisdom which has caused him to amend the error of his past dissipations and sent him, Allah willing, to our mosque?"

"Allah willing, yes. But it is I who sends him there. He is middle-aged, yet still strongheaded, slow to put his old ways behind him. It is his poor eyesight which now causes him to mistake the donkey's backside for its front."

Such is the illusory power of religious ritual and all worldly impressions, which concerned Epictetus and other men of higher knowledge and wisdom. In order to develop the perception that distinguishes reality from illusion, one must normally learn *how* to learn, to prepare the mind for the experience of perception, reflection, intuition, and illumination. A necessary first requirement may be acknowledging that we do not know what these things actually mean. In Eastern traditions, such as authentic Yoga, Zen, and Sufism, the phase of preparation is known as discipleship. This involves self-work, in some ways much more difficult than book learning. It entails questioning one's beliefs, values, biases, and assumptions, and challenging conditioning and habit. It means coming to grips with one's negative qualities—jealousy, envy, temper, greed, selfishness, and animosity. Vanity and egocentricity, the most elusive self-enemies of all, are tracked down and harmoniously uprooted to make way for more positive elements.

Humans often presume that they do not need self-work and think that they understand themselves already. Laboring in this ignorance, they attempt to evaluate and judge what is going on in the world around them. Distorted ideas are the result. Psychologist Charles Tart makes this point clear when he underscores several counterproductive assumptions prevalent in science, including this one: *We can understand the physical universe without understanding ourselves.* Tart notes that "physicists are not required to take courses in psychology or self-awareness as part of their training. . . . To put it extremely, a first-class physicist making excellent progress in the physical sciences may torture children for a hobby."[1]

And of course the physicist's (or any specialist's) quality of work may also suffer. In contrast to the assumptions that neglect the connections between psychic and physical reality, the major psychospiritual disciplines hold that one's mental and spiritual state will qualitatively influence his or her understanding of the universe. "Learning how to learn," or the period of preparation for knowledge, is analogous, in Eastern terms, to the polishing of a mirror. When one's heart and mind have been cleared of the rust (habit, prejudice, egoism, and the like) that distorts the true image of reality, then its unblemished reflection can appear. One then mirrors reality by living its truth.

While truth, reality, and knowledge are ineffable in their highest forms, sagacious persons can reflect their wisdom in their actions, speech, and works of art and literature. Some verbal examples are provided here.

> The man who gathers only the flowers (of sense pleasures), whose mind is entangled, death carries him away as a great flood a sleeping village.
>
> Buddha

> "I have sons, I have wealth": thinking thus the fool is troubled. Indeed, he himself is not his own. How can sons or wealth be his?
>
> Buddha

> There are some things in the world which are not *of* it, such as

knowledge and good deeds. A man carries what knowledge he possesses with him into the next world, and though his good deeds have passed, yet the effect of them remains in his character.

Al-Ghazzali

Men of loftier mind manifest themselves in their equitable dealings; small-minded men in their going after gain.

Confucius

To accept destiny is to face life with open eyes,
Whereas not to accept destiny is to face death blindfold.
He who is open-eyed is open-minded,
He who is open-minded is open-hearted,
He who is open-hearted is kingly,
He who is kingly is godly,
He who is godly is useful,
He who is useful is infinite,
He who is infinite is immune,
He who is immune is immortal.

Lao Tze

Do not seek death. Death will find you. But seek the road which makes death a fulfillment.

Dag Hammarskjold, *Markings*

Man's life of bondage to the world of birth and death has many causes. The root of them all is the ego, the first-begotten child of ignorance.

Shankara

In pondering the higher workings of the mind, we must inevitably consider that enigmatic subject called mysticism. Little is understood about mysticism in the West. Because of our overevaluation of logic and rationality, it is regarded with unnecessary suspicion in many quarters. Frequently (and not uncommonly among psychiatrists and psychologists) mystical states are thought of as entranced irrationality—"castles-in-the-air" aberrancy. But paradoxically, in-depth studies of mysticism by competent thinkers and scholars reveal that, far from being pathological, genuine mystical capacity is aligned with—and a sure sign of—advanced development.

Al-Ghazzali referred to mystics as "the salt which preserves human societies from decay." Hagiographies of mystical saints, as well as the achievements and words of many other individuals who attributed their insight and inspiration to mystical sources, bear out Al-Ghazzali's assertion. One needs merely to read such classical treatments as these to grasp the full scope and impact of the mystical influence in human affairs: *Mysticism*, Evelyn Underhill; *Mysticism: Sacred and Profane*, R. C. Zaehner; *Mystical Experience*, Ben-Ami Scharfstein; *Mysticism and Religion*, Robert S. Elwood; *The Varities of Religious Experience*, William James.[2]

In a recent book, *The Observing Self: Mysticism and Psychotherapy*, psychiatrist Arthur Deikman elucidates the role of mysticism in the processes of psychotherapy and development. With insight, he states that "we can think of the entire history of mysticism as the history of a science of intuitive development. . . . Its goal is understanding the reality that underlies the world of ordinary experience."[3] Deikman emphasizes that intuition is a deeply internal sense, dormant within most of us, but which can be activated under certain conditions. Mystical schools (including Eastern disciplines) specialize in the initial awakening and orientation of this sense, vis-à-vis subtle teaching input and exercising of the perceptual faculty.

The "reality underlying ordinary experience" is not accessible to the external senses. This is not to say, however, that the phenomenal world has no important role in mystical teaching. On the contrary, one's capacities are tested therein, and—providing that she or he indeed learns—everyday life becomes his proving ground. Generally, the successful learner becomes more effective in his enterprises, a by-product of his training. Getting in touch with the deeper firmament of the Self typically results in some dissolution of confusion. As Deikman notes, "The perception of that underlying reality gives meaning to individual existence and does away with the fear of death and the self-centered desires that direct the lives of most people." He then adds, "The intuition of the nature of reality marks the transition to the next stage of evolutionary development, which is the destiny of the human race. The end of that process cannot be seen."[4]

Notes

1. Charles T. Tart, "Some Assumptions of Orthodox, Western Psychology," *Transpersonal Psychologies* (New York: Harper & Row, Publishers, 1975), p. 69.
2. Evelyn Underhill, *Mysticism* (New York: E. P. Dutton & Co., 1961); R. C. Zaehner, *Mysticism: Sacred and Profane* (Oxford: Oxford University/Clarendon Press, 1961); Ben-Ami Scharfstein, *Mystical Experience* (Baltimore: Penguin Books, 1974); Robert S. Elwood, *Mysticism and Religion* (Englewood Cliffs, N.J.: Prentice-Hall, 1980); William James, *The Varieties of Religious Experience* (New York: New American Library, 1958).
3. Arthur Deikman, *The Observing Self: Mysticism and Psychotherapy* (Boston: Beacon Press, 1982).
4. Ibid., p. 41.

Afterword

A book you have probably never heard of is *The Mind in The Making*, written by an uncommonly thoughtful scholar named James Harvey Robinson and published in 1916, during World War I.[1] Along with many other people, Robinson was distressed by the various social trends that had culminated in the war: widespread unemployment and poverty, high-level political corruption, and "national arrogance, race animosity . . . and inefficiency." Robinson observed that if by "some magical transformation" men could perceive themselves and each other in qualitatively different ways, then "no inconsiderable part of the evils which now afflict society would vanish away or remedy themselves automatically."

The Mind in The Making is in some respects similar to other humanist-idealistic tracts written before and since. But unlike most, it is generally free of dogmatism and naiveté in its express purpose to assist in the making of a better world. Perhaps because he was a wartime writer, Robinson's optimism for the future was not full of florid hopes but rather was a pragmatic understanding of those mental dynamics that are the key to the actualization of an improved state for man. His book contains astute, straightforward descriptions of both the problems and potential increasing a healthier society, taken at the individual level. Unequivocally he states that the sine qua non for his task is *"to create an unprecedented attitude of mind to cope with unprecedented conditions, and to utilize unprecedented knowledge."*

Obviously Robinson knew what he and all humanitarians were up against. Every age in history is more "unprecedented" than the last in its conditions and problems but all too precedented in its essential "attitude of mind." *The Mind in The Making* targets, as does this book, limited thinking as the cause of personal and social malfunctioning. Its proposals for self-change are not set forth as formulae, nor suggested to be a novel "answer" to the question of how the malfunction can be set right. Robinson thoroughly grasped the average person's susceptibility to the negative mental contagions in the social atmosphere of his time, far more common than the common cold. He fully agreed with the Greek stoic Epictetus that "men are tormented by the opinions they have of things, rather than by the things themselves."

Like Robinson, we too are concerned with humanity's seemingly congenital resistance to necessary change and, even more alarmingly, their very inability—or refusal—to recognize their dilemma. In our view, this awakening should be the initial task of education and psychology. The "preliminary steps" (as Robinson terms them) of this process should be guided by individuals who are themselves awakened; otherwise the effort is truly "the blind leading the blind." At the outset it is beneficial for the aspiring learner to know that the task is not an easy one and that staying awake and further awakening are lifetime undertakings.

While *More Ways to Use Your Head* is, like its predecessor, *Use Your Head*, potentially useful in this respect, we must remind you that to read these books too speedily or cursorily (as you might a novel) is as futile as trying to pan for gold in a hurry; much will be lost and little or nothing gained. The substance must "sluice" in the brain slowly and be allowed to settle in the mind before it can actually be grasped. Many of the ideas and themes are subtly mixed in with more obvious concepts, requiring, perhaps, several readings. Self-observation is the method of getting at the gold within yourself. It will make you a better reader of all books as well as of your own mind.

While the Greek philosopher Socrates' "Know thyself" is the implicit basis of all self-help advice, we all know that advice differs greatly in efficacy, depending on the knowledge it possesses or lacks. In this regard we cannot recommend the writings of the brilliant thinker Idries Shah too highly. If you are willing to admit that there is more to knowing oneself than is commonly assumed, then you can certainly profit from Shah's nonpareil elucidations of personal psychology and learning principles.

And if you are ever fortunate enough to "know thyself" in the deepest sense, you will not just be using your head but fulfilling the very purpose of your being. With this ideal must go a continual caution, however: To believe that one has arrived at this state when one hasn't means that one doesn't know oneself at all and is probably not even using his or her head much.

> Understand that your time has a limit set to it. Use it, then, to advance your enlightenment; or it will be gone, and never in your power again.
>
> Marcus Aurelius

Note

1. James Harvey Robinson, *The Mind in the Making* (New York: Harper and Brothers, 1921).

Index